Rectitude

Rectitude

BEREKET ABRAHA NEGASSI

Negassi Publishing
San Francisco, California
2019

This book is a work of non-fiction. Everything written here is intended to make the world a better place by advocating for synergy, equality, social justice, and a respect for humanity and the geographical environment it inhabits.

Rectitude
© 2019 by Bereket Negassi
ISBN 978-10-97472-27-7

Editor: Leah Rubin, Your Second Pen at www.yoursecondpen.com
Cover design, interior design and layout: Tamian Wood, Beyond Design
International at www.BeyondDesignInternational.com

Author can be contacted at: bereket.abraha@gmail.com,
Facebook.com/bereketabraha
Twitter@rectitude

Table of Contents

"If you think you are too small to make a difference, you haven't spent the night with a mosquito."

African proverb quoted by the Dalai Lama.

Book 1: African Proverbs for Hope and
Balance: A Social Therapy

and

Book 2: "Corporationalism":
The End of Ideologies

Dedication

This book is dedicated to the wonderful American society formed by immigrants who were citizens from all parts of the world and arrived here at different times. This society is welcoming, humble, polite and empathetic, in general. I would like to encourage appreciation of these values to continue throughout all generations to come.

My humble advice is to not shake a beehive outside your door and then spend money to protect your home from nervous bees. There should be smarter ways to live in harmony with your neighbors or guests who seek refuge.

Acknowledgments

I would like to thank my professors and the nursing department at the University of San Francisco for their patience, knowledge, and guidance.

I would like to thank HealthRIGHT 360 for providing me with the opportunity to think about a message of hope and balance.

I would like to thank the people residing in Walden House and wish them all the best, from the bottom of my heart.

I would like to thank my Mother for everything she did.

I would like to thank my wife for her input and support, which was beyond words.

I would like to thank my kids for always giving me a reason to smile and be grateful.

I would like to thank my family and friends for their support and prayers.

I would like to thank my editor, Leah Rubin.

I would like to thank Tamian Wood for shining this book with her sprinkles of art.

And, most importantly,
I would like to thank God for his grace.

Introduction

Humans are beautiful beings who are intertwined with each other by a healthy social order. The order is set for the purpose of satisfying needs, from physiological to self-actualization, according to Maslow's hierarchy of needs. The social order is directed by politics according to cultural, geographical, economical and/or spiritual norms.

In this book, I've compiled two seemingly different concepts related to social therapy and social order within our great American society. The two books raise the concern of ideological social values in shaping our macroeconomic policy in order to achieve social justice for all. In order to fulfill the issues of social justice, we need to have a healthy individual citizen that can contribute to the collective American beneficence using proverbs created by African ancestors. The social order can be better directed by policies formed under the banner of what I call "Corporationalism."

The two stories I wrote in this book are the result of profound experiences during my childhood in Africa, my life as a citizen of these great United States, and my education at the University of San Francisco. I hope these stories will inspire people to believe that we are not just ants and grasshoppers who line up to work and come back home every day. We humans are souls. We are spirits connected and intertwined as a society on this beautiful place we call earth and in this amazing country called America.

Book 1

African Proverbs for Hope and Balance: A Social Therapy

Chapter 1

Social Interaction Using Afro-therapy

I am a nursing student at the University of San Francisco, one of the many hundreds of Jesuit Universities throughout the United States. The reason I joined this institution was because I made a promise to my mother, who lost her battle to breast cancer in 1997, that I would fight against this cancer until I die. I am called to be an oncology nurse in order to help women (and men) fight this horrible disease.

This is an observational study. It needs further assessment and consideration to add grace to the amazing work of all healthcare providers, their teams, and management, as they go hand in hand to ease the suffering of humankind.

During my psychiatric/community health rotation, I was assigned to a great historical facility called Walden House. There, I was fortunate to work with ex-prisoners and recovering drug addicts. Clients there are expected to reunite with society after ninety days of help and support. The service is provided by HealthRIGHT 360 in San Francisco, CA.

Walden House was founded in 1969 and named after *Walden Two*, a controversial utopian novel written by behavioral psychologist B.F. Skinner in 1948. At that time, his novel could have been considered science fiction because science-based methods did not yet exist for altering people's behavior. These methods are now known as Applied Behavioral Analysis (ABA).

Walden House began with twenty-five substance abuser runaway teens in the Haight-Ashbury district of San Francisco. I went to the building located close to Alamo square near Hayes Valley. It is a majestic building; the main meeting hall looks like a former church, with paintings and artworks on the wall that reflect a spiritual influence.

A significant number of citizens are housed and get help in this facility. The clients have a unique set of rules to abide by during their ninety-day stay in order to ensure their success. They are aware of their problems and work diligently to change their lives.

There are some clients who find it difficult to finish the three-month program, but the majority are successful and receive assistance in finding a job and housing, so that they can live independent and productive lives. I invite anyone who reads this to help this facility run by HealthRIGHT 360 to transform the clients on their journeys. They need role models who survived addictions and trauma and can inspire the clients with their successes. They need a lot of spiritual help. They need financial help. I would like to take this opportunity to thank HealthRIGHT 360 and their team for helping to transform people's lives.

I was assigned with two of my student colleagues and we were led by a clinical professor from the University of San Francisco for our practical assignment during the community health clinical rotation. Our professor observed and guided us, while the three of us chose how to lead our groups independently of one another. One of my colleagues led groups and taught them about nutrition and living a healthy lifestyle. The other colleague's topics were diabetes and CPR. I led groups using the steps that led to this book. We supported each other, exchanged ideas and suggestions for our plans with the clients, and reported our findings to our professor.

Our goal was to learn how to lead groups so that ideas could be exchanged regarding common problems and coping mechanisms within a community.

The first step I took was to ask clients for the areas of support they needed. I found out that the majority of my subjects wanted to learn how to keep their hope and balance.

One of the social justice issues that needs to be addressed properly is the cycle of prisons and the mentally ill. In addition to governmental structural changes, health care institutions can do their part as well. But currently, America is very rough with its mentally ill prisoners.

Stigma and separation exacerbate the problem. These prisoners/patients are left to involve themselves with the successive commitment of crimes and addiction to various forms of drugs and alcohol. In order to help these people and to save the cost of care, they need to be given the message of hope and balance. I propose the use of African proverbs in therapy.

Africa can deliver the message of hope and balance to our fellow Americans who are alienated from their society because they have various problems. They can use African folk stories. They can reconnect with other humans that created a way to reconcile with themselves, attain resilience, and live in prosperity with nature.

African ancestors, led by wise elders, transferred life-long knowledge to the new generations using stories and proverbs. It is easy to see that the proverbs have stories related to animals, plants, and nature which show the Africans' attachment to their environment. However, these proverbs are not perfect; some even look down on women. That, unfortunately, is still a problem in the hierarchy of African society.

Method: I applied these proverbs to moderate a preferably smaller group of ten clients at the most. I typed, cut, and gave a proverb to each of the participants who read them and meditated on them. They understood and interpreted them according to their individual points of view. There were only two questions asked. The first was: "What does the proverb mean?" The second question was: "What does this proverb mean to you?" There were no wrong answers and there were no judgments made.

Clients agreed to verbal contracts that stated: "All participants will agree to not share information outside the group and will agree to use the personal information they hear with respect. In order to maintain privacy, no recording of any kind is allowed. Clients will treat each other with respect. Clients agree to speak in turn, and no interrupting is allowed. Clients are free to speak about what they believe and try not to use their wisdom to attack or harass each other. They will explain their view about the core message of the proverb. They will listen and react to other members' interpretations."

I was the person who led the group and I agreed to not participate in correcting a client's interpretations. As the leader, I had to be calm and allow the group to resolve their problems, unless the situation got out of hand. I participated in moderating conversations, not influencing views. Scores were subjective and given according to the expectation of the organization that runs the facility, based on company policy and procedure. Scores were coded and documented. The document remained the property of the organization. The organization will create policy on how and how much to share, and with whom they share in the future.

Outcome: Based upon answers to a survey given at the end of each session, participants from various races and backgrounds were surprised that simple and overlooked proverbs from poor Africa could provide valuable messages of hope and balance. Clients were surprised, and they expressed their feelings towards Africa and its elders. Clients from various races made connections with Africa. Most seemed to acknowledge that Africa is in their hearts and that they see Africa as their origin, no matter where they were from.

I observed that the participant groups grew from around ten the first day to over sixty after two sessions. Some of the participants told me the proverbs changed their lives by showing them a way to look at life differently. They admitted to opening up and discussing effectively more than what they would with their therapists. They were inspired by the vast African wisdom, the awareness of African societies, their potential impact on social life, and their relationship with nature, which seems to be fading in American society. They realized they were not the only ones who suffer from problems related to hope and balance, and they promised to use the proverbs as an additional mechanism for coping.

There were some conflicts that occurred. Some clients used the medium to address personal issues with disrespect. Some clients didn't give a chance for others to voice their views. Some of them thought they were targeted through the conversations and were angry, as a result. Some clients thought it was a waste of time and tried to push others to leave. Some showed me (as the group leader) disrespect and breached the verbal contract. Normally, a breach of this contract would have resulted in removal of the participant from the session. It was a close call but did not get out of hand at that time.

Assessment: Healthcare organizations, support groups, and even families and friends can use the proverbs to assess each individual for his/her ability to interact with others. We can classify and help each participant based on a social interaction scale.

The Scale

Inattentive Nonreactive	Inattentive Interested	Attentive Nonreactive	Attentive Reactive	Attentive Dominating	Overattentive Nonreactive
0	1	2	3	4	5

The scale used was based on 5 consecutive sessions for each client and results were recorded.

The groups were held voluntarily without preconditions. As the group leader, I sat in a median place surrounded by clients. I started the conversation with a greeting and introduction, and I allowed the clients to briefly introduce themselves. Then I explained what Afro-therapy is and its goal. I continued with an explanation of the verbal contract and made sure the clients either agreed or left the group immediately. I remained calm and let the clients have conversations, but I did not participate in interpreting the proverbs or providing my interpretation as to the final meaning of the proverbs.

A code was assigned to each client (such as A, B, C, etc.,) instead of using that client's name. I gave a score and the reason for that score. Later, assessments were made. Final scores were given as an average after 5 consecutive sessions, in order to provide time for me to know and understand individual behaviors and avoid biases. Scores were documented and remain the property of the organization.

Conclusion: Results indicated that clients were observed showing various manifestations of social interactions. Diverse behaviors were exhibited based on each client's interactions and related to their personal experience, whether they could control them or not.

Clients were observed showing that their behaviors were influenced by the environments in which they grew up or joined later in their lives. Clients were observed expressing emotions such as anger and regret. Some cried and expressed depressed behavior the entire time. Some clients began to explore or face their past and recognized where they began to be lost and what led to their problems.

Some of them would uncontrollably run the show by wanting everyone to only listen to what they had to say. Others would stay dormant and continue to just listen to the interactions of others. Some clients would argue, trying to create conflict between themselves and others.

Recommendation: The initial problem of addiction is influenced by spiritual distress with physiological consequences, as indicated by clients during a survey. They stated that they "needed a message of hope and balance", and that the way out is to address their spiritual issues.

According to Maslow's hierarchy of needs, in addition to physiological consequences that can be treated according to clinical diagnosis, if clients come to terms with hope and balance in their lives, they tend to admit drug use and addiction. That admission is the most important step in the healing process. Then, with help, they can achieve further in gaining balance and living with hope and prosperity.

The cognitive, attention, listening and expressive abilities, along with the conflict resolution and tolerance of the clients, can be further assessed by the behaviors they manifested. As a result, this scale helps providers with additional assessments on how clients might react when they are mixed with society, in general. Clients are also assessed for their respect of self and others (including authority), and their ability to seek help and support properly. This scale is not a diagnosis of any disease.

Additional studies can be made regarding cognition, neurological diseases, processes, and symptoms related to Alzheimer's, dementia, or drug and alcohol induced delirium, confusion and other changes in behavior.

Afro-therapy scale of interpretations

Inattentive Nonreactive	Inattentive Interested	Attentive Nonreactive	Attentive Reactive	Attentive Dominating	Overattentive Nonreactive
0	1	2	3	4	5

1. Clients who scored 0 and 5 need further assessment before they get back to a larger community.
2. Clients who scored 1 and 4 need close observation and guidance before they get back to a larger community.
3. Clients who scored 2 and 3 are ready to go back to a larger community with guidance.

In the chapters that follow, you will find the proverbs used in this study. The descriptions are my personal interpretations, not necessarily the right interpretations. I wrote what I would have said if I had been a participant of the target group, instead of the leader.

chapter notes:

Chapter 2

African Proverbs on Wisdom

Wisdom is related to the time it takes for a person to acquire applicable experience of the knowledge a community values and highly regards. Knowledge can be either acquired from the environment or transferred through genetics—the idea that a person, who experienced and lived a particular life, can explain wisdom better.

Here are some of my examples of wisdom acquired through a life experience. For Americans, who have one of the largest prisoner populations in the world, no one can tell about life in a prison more than a prisoner. Who can tell me about stars more than an astronomer? No one can explain how difficult life is on the streets better than a homeless person. Also, if I want to know about poverty, I know who to ask.

If I seek advice on how devastating a war is, I would go to soldiers who experienced combat. You would go to wise elders if you want to know about your history and culture. People don't usually elect a non-politician to lead a political process. However, we now have people like Donald Trump in the Oval

Office representing everything American. President Trump is a successful businessman, and his policies might be as good as every president before him. But he is not a unifying figure. If I go to any other country in the world, I would tell people that America is a wonderful country with hardworking and generous people who are being led by the wrong figure.

Don't try to forecast monitory policy if you are not an economist.

Leave weather predictions to meteorologists.

Don't dare to be more Catholic than the Pope.

A wise person is careful of what he or she says. African elders are known to be calm, patient, courageous and humble. They listen before they talk. They carefully observe before they advise. They assess people's attitudes and they think before they say anything.

Confidence and contents spoken during public speech is one method by which Africans can tell who is wise. A wise person is recognized mostly at gatherings like weddings, cultural and religious events, ceremonies, and festivals. Wisdom is the quality that makes us better than other animals.

Wisdom is a power capable of keeping the qualities of philosophy and math, as well as those of body and spirit, in balance. Only the wise person is capable of doing this. Wisdom is the only power that can change the world into becoming better or worse.

Every country has its own wise people. They are role models that shape their nation. Without wisdom, there is no peace. Without wisdom, there is no constitution. Without wisdom, there is no rule of law. Without wisdom, there is no spirituality.

Here are some African proverbs related to wisdom.

- *Wisdom is wealth.*
  Swahili

- *Wisdom is like the majestic baobab tree; no one individual can embrace it.*
  Akan (Ghana)

- *The fool speaks, the wise man listens.*
  Ethiopia

- *Wisdom does not come overnight.*
  Somalia

- *The heart of the wise man lies quiet like limpid water.*
  Cameroon

- *Wisdom is like fire. People take it from others.*
  Hema (DRC)

- *Only a wise person can solve a difficult problem.*
  Akan (Ghana)

- *Knowledge without wisdom is like water in the sand.*
  Guinea

- *In the moment of crisis, the wise build bridges and the foolish build dams.*
  Nigeria

- *If you are filled with pride, then you will have no room for wisdom.*
    Africa

- *A wise person will always find a way.*
    Tanzania

- *Nobody is born wise.*
    Africa

- *A man who uses force is afraid of reasoning.*
    Kenya

- *Wisdom is not like money to be tied up and hidden.*
    Akan (Ghana)

chapter notes:

Chapter 3

African Proverbs on Learning

Learning is one way of acquiring wisdom. People can learn from many things: mistakes, achievements, schools, books, and through conversations, etc., using all senses and the conscious brain.

We have to be open to new knowledge without limits. People can use learning for various purposes. They learn to harm or do good. People can learn to exceed positivity or to scale down negativity. They can learn to grow for betterment or unlearn to stop the madness they acquired. Therefore, we have to use every opportunity to learn a lesson.

Africans believe learning is an enrichment of the soul. Learning is the food of the soul, as the soul can only live by feeding on knowledge. The soul could starve to death when there is lack of knowledge and then we would become incomplete; the soul is what completes us as humans. Without a soul we are just bones and flesh. Therefore, we need to enrich our humanness. We are better than other animals because our brain is created to retain, grow, apply, and store knowledge and wisdom.

African elders advise their children to continue to learn, so that they can emancipate themselves from a dead soul, because a broken soul cannot achieve anything. They call that person a fool. Learning can lift people out of poverty. It is the ticket to win hearts and rule souls. Learning is a source of curiosity and creativity.

The wise are always humble. The wise do not refrain from teaching others. The wise don't use their knowledge to harm the environment. The wise don't use their knowledge to start conflict and war. The wise learn from their mistakes. The wise will not make the same mistakes over and over again.

The wise are very few in number and they are capable of ruling their world from behind the scenes. The wise are the ones who are ashamed when they are represented by fools. The wise are ashamed when fools becomes leaders. They would do what it takes to correct the mistakes made by foolish leaders. When there are a lot of wise people, we have less divorces, less conflicts, less prisons, less fools, and more gratitude, goodwill, respect, and the rule of law.

When we have more wise people, we have more science and math, better healthcare, and more discovery and creativity.

When we have more wise people, we use less proverbs, because telling fools their mistakes directly can have bad consequences. If you tell a fool his or her mistake directly, they will be offended. They would try to cover them with other mistakes or they would oppose criticism.

Here are some proverbs regarding learning.

- *Learning expands great souls.*
  Namibia

- *To get lost is to learn the way.*
  Africa

- *By crawling a child learns to stand.*
  Africa

- *If you close your eyes to facts, you will learn through accidents.*
  Africa

- *He who learns, teaches.*
  Ethiopia

- *Wealth, if you use it, comes to an end; learning, if you use it, increases.*
  Swahili

- *By trying often, the monkey learns to jump from the tree.*
  Buganda

- *You always learn a lot more when you lose than when you win.*
  Africa

- *You learn how to cut down trees by cutting them down.*
  Bateke

- *The wise create proverbs for fools to learn, not to repeat.*
  Africa

- *By the time a fool has learned the game, the players have dispersed.*
  Ashanti (Ghana)

- *What you help a child to love can be more important than what you help him to learn.*
  Africa

- *One who causes others misfortune also teaches them wisdom.*
  Africa

- *You do not teach the paths of the forest to an old gorilla.*
  Congo

- *What you learn is what you die with.*
  Africa

- *Instruction in youth is like engraving in stone.*
  Morocco

- *Traveling is learning.*
  Kenya

- *When you follow in the path of your father, you learn to walk like him.*
  Ashanti (Ghana)

- *Ears that do not listen to advice, accompany the head when it is chopped off.*
    Africa

- *Advice is a stranger; if he's welcome, he stays for the night; if not, he leaves the same day.*
    Malagasy

- *Where there are experts there will be no lack of learners.*
    Swahili

chapter notes:

Chapter 4

African Proverbs on Peace and Leadership

Africans value peace just like other societies in the world. They lived in peace and harmony with nature for generations until the Europeans arrived on their soil.

There is a kind of lie or stigma when the media portrays that Africa has had more wars and poverty than any continent on the globe; that's incorrect.

Africa is a rich continent with minerals and oils in the ground, and blessings on the ground and in its sky. They have unique customary and elder laws that govern societies through conflict resolution techniques. Africans have developed medicine and various forms of healing methods. They are unique with deep-rooted social support. Africans are known for respect of family and friendship. They are unique in acknowledging their belief in the creator. That's how they maintain and value peace and harmony.

Africa had actually been a peaceful continent for generations until strangers put their footsteps there. Devastating wars came to Africa with slavery-related businesses, colonization, and the search and exploitation of its natural resources. Africans knew and lived in harmony with nature and amongst tribes before then.

More devastating wars in the far east, Europe, Asia, and the Americas were recorded in history than Africans experienced in their lifetimes. Conflicts were orchestrated and exported to Africa. It was and is a victim of extended and proxy rivalry between superpowers.

Peace is not only related to countries or societies, it begins within one's self. People who live in internal peace and harmony are free from depression, abuse, and conflicts, and can live healthy for a long time.

Africans believe when peace prevails, animals can freely move, plants can grow and expand, and the sky can produce a healthy rain. When peace prevails, children can grow playful and healthy and elders become hopeful and tell their stories. When peace prevails, land can produce plenty, and animals can give blessings. When peace prevails, men and women fall in love and exchange the pomegranate as a symbol of their love. When peace prevails, patients heal and the dead get a well-deserved honor.

Leadership has a lot of meaning for African societies. Women are the first examples; they know how to manage their limited resources in order to raise a family. We have historical female and male leaders that elevated Africans to power and changed the world. We can mention Cleopatra, Nefertiti, Queen Makeda, Queen Judith, Aminatu, Nandi, and Ranavalona. They are the best the world can be proud of.

We have Nelson Mandela, Robert Mugabe, Muamar Ghadafi, Isaias Afeworki, Haile Selassie, Abiy Ahmad, Ziad Bare, Jomo Kenyatta, Kenneth Kaunda, Samora Machel, Thomas Sankara, Patrice Lumumba, Menelik, Ellen Johnson Sirleaf, Julius Nyerere, Kwame Nkrumah, from recent history; and Mansa Musa, King Shaka, Yaa Asantewa, King Ramesses, Amenhotep, Nzinga, King Ezana, and many more.

Leadership is acquired with wisdom and age, when length of conscious longevity in this world prepares someone with this ability. Leadership starts with self. A person should manage the balance between ego and the environment. Africans believe one's ability to lead has some genetic component, and they would follow a good leader's descendants.

The quality of leadership is tested with a person's empathy, compassion, and words. A leader naturally is graceful, yet firm. A leader is merciful and smart. When a country has a good leader, the earth will give more fruit, the wild animals flourish, and flowers bloom.

Africa has seen great leaders as well as cruel ones; but Africans mostly want someone who unites them. A leader should be a person who always learns lessons. Wise leaders bring peace and harmony, they don't exercise power just because they can. They have faith in God. They respect others and are respected by other societies. They are feared by their enemies and loved by their allies.

Leadership starts and ends with self-control. Naturally, there are many kinds of leaders, such as charismatic, laissez-faire, collective, democratic, or dictatorial. One can have the qualities of all kinds of leadership habits, or just one of them. However, leadership is evaluated by the result.

Quality of leadership is measured by forming and managing effective structures, with a clear vision and objective. Leaders should line up people behind them because they need to make sure tasks are done when they are not around. Great leaders should prepare successors, so that their legacy continues.

They should make sure minorities are respected and majorities are getting their rightful place. They should sacrifice their energy and time for their country (or group) and strive to create a just society.

Below are some proverbs related to peace and self- or follower-based leadership.

- *Peace is costly, but it is worth the expense.*
  Kenya

- *War has no eyes.*
  Swahili

- *When a king has good counselors, his reign is peaceful.*
  Ashanti (Ghana)

- *Peace does not make a good ruler.*
  Botswana

- *A fight between grasshoppers is a joy to the crow.*
  Lesotho

- *There can be no peace without understanding.*
  Senegal

- *Milk and honey have different colors, but they share the same house peacefully.*
  Africa

- *If you can't resolve your problems in peace, you can't solve war.*
  Somalia

- *When there is peace in the country, the chief does not carry a shield.*
  Uganda

- *When two elephants fight, it is the grass that gets trampled.*
  Swahili

- *Speak softly and carry a big stick; you will go far.*
  West African

- *He who thinks he is leading and has no one following him is only taking a walk.*
  Malawi

- *An army of sheep led by a lion can defeat an army of lions led by a sheep.*
  Ghana

- *He who is destined for power does not have to fight for it.*
  Uganda

- *Do not forget what it is to be a sailor because of being a captain yourself.*
  Tanzania

- *Without a leader, black ants are confused.*
  Uganda

- *He who refuses to obey cannot command.*
  Kenya

- *He who fears the sun will not become chief.*
  Uganda

- *A large chair does not make a king.*
  Sudan

- *Because he lost his reputation, he lost a kingdom.*
  Ethiopia

- *Where a woman rules, streams run uphill.*
  Ethiopia

- *A leader who does not take advice is not a leader.*
  Kenya

- *If the cockroach wants to rule over the chicken, then it must hire the fox as a bodyguard.*
  Sierra Leone

chapter notes:

Chapter 5

African Proverbs on Unity and Community

Unity is celebrated in any African country. The Organization of African Unity is one of the most remarkable projects ever created by African leaders. Through this organization, Africans raised their voices until each country achieved independence.

There are a lot of celebrated leaders that helped the dream of independence become a reality. These were charismatic leaders who made a difference. To name a few, there were: Dr. Kwame Nkrumah of Ghana, Modibo Keita of Mali, Gamal Abdul Nasser of Egypt, Sekou Touré of Guinea, Julius Nyerere of Tanzania, Ben Bella of Algeria, Emperor Haile Selassie of Ethiopia, William Tubman of Liberia, Abubakar Tafawa Balewa of Nigeria, Nnamdi Azikiwe of Nigeria, and Jomo Kenyatta of Kenya.

These leaders were inspired by Pan Africanism, a struggle to make Africans perceive that they were not savages and were capable of choosing their destiny; if they were united as one country, they could rule the world. There is no place in the world without people of the African diaspora, but these people suffered as a result of slavery and were subjected to deliberate brutalities.

In order to achieve independence, African leaders formed a union so they could advocate for and achieve political independence.

Long before independence, longer still before slavery, Africans formed civilizations that changed the world. These civilizations were accomplished through unity. When tribes unite, they are stronger and richer; and when they separate, they become weaker and vulnerable. Africans learn to live in harmony with nature through their unity. African elders advise that unity starts with friends, family, and villages and continues all the way to the national level in order to win a common goal.

Another important factor of unity is that there is no community without unity. A community without unity is just a bunch of humans. Communities share the same traits; they support each other during good and bad times.

Communities are identified by their common beliefs. Africa advises America to strengthen its sense of community. The sense of community that I observe in California is not promising. People are afraid to leave kids play outside or send them to school alone. Communities are divided based on race, class, religion and where they are from.

I see no problem with preferring to be with people like yourself. However, it is bad when you treat others as strangers or potential adversaries. People should start knocking on doors and introducing themselves to their neighbors. They should set aside time to meet and celebrate their community. Trust is the pillar of a community. The threats to our sense of community are racism, sexism, fanaticism, materialism, criminality, self-centeredness, fear and more.

Communities need to help the poor, homeless, mentally ill, prisoners, alcoholics and drug addicts, single parents, those who are alone and isolated, and the people who are there to give service, such as the teachers, nurses, police, firefighters, religious and community leaders, and politicians.

Leadership without community is senseless. Therefore, community is a precondition to leadership. Leaders are products of a good community. We have examples of communities that help and support their members. Those communities can be religious, ethnic, work-related, or associations.

Those communities are a great source of support for people who can use them. Nurses always search and recommend community support groups for various needs. We recommend patients who have rare diseases to join groups that have similar diagnoses.

We recommend alcoholics and drug addicts to support groups. We, as health care providers, join various support groups that help us support and achieve our common goals.

Africans are known for forming and continuing with community groups based on various visions. It is difficult for Africans to live by themselves. We tend to join any group to talk with, eat with, or share our happiness during good times and support during our times of grief.

Here are some proverbs regarding unity and community.

- *Unity is strength, division is weakness.*
  Swahili

- *Sticks in a bundle are unbreakable.*
  Bondei

- *It takes a village to raise a child.*
  Africa

- *Cross the river in a crowd and the crocodile won't eat you.*
  Africa

- *Many hands make light work.*
  Tanzania (Haya)

- *Where there are many, nothing goes wrong.*
  Swahili

- *Two ants do not fail to pull one grasshopper.*
  Tanzania

- *A single bracelet does not jingle.*
  Congo

- *A single stick may smoke, but it will not burn.*
  Africa

- *If you want to go quickly, go alone. If you want to go far, go together.*
  Africa

chapter notes

Chapter 6

African Proverbs on Family

America has a lot to learn about family values from Africa. In my perception, Americans call it a family if everyone is blood related. Family structure and bonding is different from the African perspective. We probably find similar bonding within similar groups of American service members.

The African family is formed like a web or a wave. It starts with an elder or a respected role model at the center. That person forms the nuclear family, which consists of the grandparents, the parents, the children, and the brothers and sisters of the parents and their children. This bond goes all the way to the bigger community.

Family is formed by people who grew up together and lived in the same neighborhood. Family is formed by people who once were total strangers, sons and daughters of our parent's friends, coworkers, soldiers deployed in the same place for a while, volunteers and workers from other countries, and most importantly, neighbors.

This happens because African tribes don't move very much; they feel very connected to their land. They tend to stay in one area for generations or they move en masse when there is a natural or man-made disaster. As a result, members of tribes know each other and treat each other as family.

I remember asking my mother who, among the kids my age, were really my cousins. She told me about a lady who gave birth at the same time as her in the same hospital and became her best friend. For a long time, I couldn't tell if her kids were my cousins. Family has no boundary and ethnicity; it is not limited by religious similarities or differences.

Ideally, families are there to support each other and spend holidays and other ceremonies together. They visit the sick, gather to bury the dead, and pray for the ones who need it. They connect their members to help them find jobs and provide opportunities. Sometimes people call that nepotism. They become mentors and volunteer to help when needed.

It is normal for families to fight a lot. However, it is not normal for families to abuse and deliberately hurt their members and inflict physical or spiritual pain upon them. It is okay to be jealous, but not okay to try to take away a member's blessings. It is okay to gossip, but not fine to cause emotional pain. There should be limits to everything we do with each other.

When we need resolution for any conflicts, we tend to go to the elders for consultations. African families do not choose elders; elders prevail. In order to be an elder, the person should have the qualities of leadership and grace. That person should treat everyone equally and fairly. The term "elder" is not an indication of age; it is an indication of wisdom.

Here are some proverbs regarding family.

- *A family is like a forest, when you are outside it is dense. when you are inside you see that each tree has its place.*
  Africa

- *A united family eats from the same plate.*
  Buganda

- *A family tie is like a tree, it can bend but it cannot break.*
  Africa

- *If I am in harmony with my family, that's success.*
  Ute, Native American

- *Brothers love each other when they are equally rich.*
  Africa

- *Dine with a stranger but save your love for your family.*
  Ethiopia

- *There is no fool who is disowned by his family.*
  Africa

- *Home affairs are not talked about on the public square.*
  Africa

- *If relatives help each other, what evil can hurt them?*
  ### *Africa*

- *He who earns calamity, eats it with his family.*
  ### *Africa*

- *The old woman looks after the child to grow its teeth and the young one in turn looks after the old woman when she loses her teeth.*
  ### *Akan (Ghana, Ivory Coast)*

- *When brothers fight to the death, a stranger inherits their father's estate.*
  ### *Ibo*

- *Children are the reward of life.*
  ### *Africa*

chapter notes:

Chapter 7

African Proverbs on Friendship

Social science defines humans as social animals. I argue we are different because we are not only flesh and blood, but we are made up of a spirit as well. Friendship is a relationship that occurs when the two spirits form a special bond.

We understand that life without a friend will lead to loneliness, helplessness, and depression, at the least. Lack of friends probably will lead to cruelty, displeasure, anger, uneasiness, and lack of empathy or compassion. Friends are the ones who are present in one's life, for better or worse.

They are present during happiness and sadness. A friend who is happy within when you are successful is hard to find. Friends are needed during troubling times. "A friend in need is a friend indeed." This expression is a good way of describing friendship in American society. The word "need" implies both the material and psychological value of benefits earned.

A friend based only on need and benefit is mostly rejected in African society, because Africans think that when the need is fulfilled, the friendship will be gone. Africans believe that the strength of friendship can be extended to the point of sacrificing one's life for another. Friendship transcends generations. That's why you can't tell if the children of friends are brothers or cousins.

We can experience the strength of a friendship when wealth is reduced; i.e., the amount of money you possess is inversely proportionate to the quality of friend you have. This type of friendship is possible in American society, too. We can find friends among the communities of the homeless, the impoverished, minorities, immigrants, vulnerable societies (in particular, Jewish, Muslim, Native American, African American, the military, fire fighters, labor unions, children, and so on).

It is often difficult for the rich to find true friends, because money and other material wealth can get caught in between relationships. My suggestion for the wealthy is to learn to give to the poor, to be more spiritual, visit places such as Africa, the far east, or anywhere there is poverty, so that they can discover there is more to the qualities of human society than wealth.

People may prefer to be friends with pets because animals will not judge them. Instead, most of them wait and stay where they are left, show emotions, and give love.

Next are some proverbs regarding friendship.

- *To be without a friend is to be poor indeed.*
  Tanzania

- *Hold a true friend with both hands.*
  Africa

- *The friends of our friends are our friends.*
  Congo

- *A friend is someone you share the path with.*
  Africa

- *Show me your friend and I will show you your character.*
  Africa

- *Return to old watering holes for more than water; friends and dreams are there to meet you.*
  Africa

- *Between true friends even water drunk together is sweet enough.*
  Africa

- *A small house will hold a hundred friends.*
  Africa

- *A close friend can become a close enemy.*
  Africa

- *If your friend is like honey, don't lick all of it.*
  Egypt

- *What visits you is what eats you.*
  Bemba

- *An onion shared with a friend tastes like roast lamb.*
  Egypt

- *Your friend's heart is a wilderness.*
  Ki Kaonde

- *When mosquitoes work, they bite and then they sing.*
  Malawi

- *Friendship doubles joy and halves grief.*
  Egypt

- *A married couple is neither enemies nor friends.*
  Somalia

- *An intelligent foe is better than a stupid friend.*
  Senegal

- *A friend who visits you when you are suffering is your best friend.*
  Rwanda

- *Every rose has a thorn as its friend.*
  Morocco

- *Don't be like a shadow: a constant companion, but not a comrade.*
  Madagascar

- *The prickly branches of the palm tree do not show preference even to friends.*
  Ghana

- *Bad friends will prevent you from having good friends.*
  Gabon

chapter notes:

Chapter 8

African Proverbs on Money, Wealth, Riches, and Poverty

Money and wealth have a higher place in African hierarchy. Africans see money as a factor that created classes and destroyed a way of living, because they used to share the wealth the earth provided equally and fairly among members of the tribes. Africans were the first of the world's civilizations to introduce money for trade when they formed bigger cities.

The society got forcefully and deliberately divided with tribal and religious lines to make it easier for the European colonial rule. The class differences were encouraged by the rulers by mostly giving the majorities power over the minorities... one of the seemingly endless reasons for conflicts. Africans have struggled to narrow class differences with strong determination ever since independence. We are still very far behind and have a long way to go in narrowing the wealth gap.

One of the reasons for the failure of wealth disparity is that politicians rejected learning from their rich culture and simply copied and adopted European ideologies (many of which didn't even help the European society). Africans fought on one side or another of communism and capitalism during the Cold War. They still have a hard time with narrowing their ideological differences and reconciling with devastations.

In American societies, the class division has led to civil war, trade disputes, segregation, inequality, displacements, and unjust legal systems that result in diminishing checks and balances of the government. As a result, lower class Americans tend to oppose the higher class.

Some of these manifestations are described by frustrations against the 1 percent having more wealth than the 99 percent. Frustrated citizens came out to cause violent oppositions during the economic downturn of 2007-2009.

Wealth disparity has been experienced by societies within all world civilizations throughout time. It will continue to pose a challenge to the world order. Therefore, Africans created proverbs regarding money and wealth so that they can have conversations and debates regarding this issue.

Here are some proverbs regarding wealth.

- *Make money but don't let money make you.*
  Tanzania

- *It is no shame at all to work for money.*
  Africa

- *He who loves money must labor.*
  Mauritania

- *By labor comes wealth.*
  Yoruba

- *Poverty is slavery.*
  Somalia

- *One cannot both feast and become rich.*
  Ashanti

- *One cannot count on riches.*
  Somalia

- *Money is sharper than the sword.*
  Ashanti

- *A man's wealth may be superior to him.*
  Cameroon

- *The rich are always complaining.*
  Zulu

- *The wealth which enslaves the owner isn't wealth.*
  Yoruba

- *The poor man and the rich man do not play together.*
  Ashanti

- *Lack of money is lack of friends; if you have money at your disposal, every dog and goat will claim to be related to you.*
  Yoruba

- *With wealth one wins a woman.*
  Uganda

- *Dogs do not actually prefer bones to meat; it is just that no one ever gives them meat.*
  Akan (Ghana)

- *A real family eats the same cornmeal.*
  Bayombe

- *If your cornfield is far from your house, the birds will eat your corn.*
  Congo

- *Money can't talk, yet it can make lies look true.*
  South Africa

- *Money is not the medicine against death.*
  Ghana

- *He who receives a gift does not measure.*
  Africa

- *Much wealth brings many enemies.*
  Swahili

- *There is no one who became rich because he broke a holiday, no one became fat because he broke a fast.*
  Ethiopia

- *What you give you get, ten times over.*
  Yoruba

- *Greed loses what it has gained.*
  Africa

- *You become wise when you begin to run out of money.*
  Ghana

- *If ten cents do not go out, it does not bring in one thousand dollars.*
  Ghana

- *You should not hoard your money and die of hunger.*
  Ghana

- *Wealth diminishes with usage; learning increases with use.*
  Nigeria

- *Wisdom is not like money to be tied up and hidden.*
  Akan (Ghana)

- *Having a good discussion is like having riches.*
  Kenya

- *Knowledge is better than riches.*
  Cameroon

- *You must act as if it is impossible to fail.*
  Ashanti

- *Do not let what you cannot do tear from your hands what you can.*
  Ashanti

chapter notes:

Chapter 9

African Proverbs on Beauty

Africa is known for beautiful landscapes, different kinds of flora and fauna, its breathtaking environment, and rich natural resources. Africa is known for ethnic diversity and it's beautiful and colorful women with special costumes and exquisite jewelry.

Africa is a population of all races: we have blacks, whites, and browns, who uses various methods to show off their identities. They have unique piercings, tattoos, and hair braids.

Africans express beauty through music, poetry, dance, and various rituals. However, beauty comes with a catch. Beauty can be internal or superficial, temporary or permanent. The beautiful one is the one people fight for; but there is a price to pay. The beautiful one is the one who is in favor with people. The beautiful one can control the powerful. One example of this is Cleopatra, who was one of the best queens Africa had and who won over Caesar and saved her kingdom. Africans are afraid of the most beautiful women; they perceive them as attractive to everyone but fear they may bring risk with them. Africans know they have to pay an arm and leg to own and preserve the beauty.

The beautiful woman is sometimes associated with deceiving the foolish lover, who has no choice but to submit and be taken advantage of. It may be difficult for a beautiful woman to settle with someone. Because she keeps looking for the best man, she may find that no one is marrying her and it becomes too late. The beautiful woman is vulnerable to abuse and rape. She is the one whom others are jealous of and she is the subject of gossip. As a result, it's likely that she may lose confidence.

Here are some proverbs regarding beauty.

- *One who plants grapes by the roadside and one who marries a pretty woman share the same problem.*
  Ethiopia

- *Beautiful from behind, ugly in front.*
  Uganda

- *The skin of the leopard is beautiful, but not his heart.*
  Baluba

- *Ugliness with a good character is better than beauty.*
  Nigeria

- *A beautiful one hurts the heart.*
  Africa

- *Anyone who sees beauty and does not look at it will soon be poor.*
  Yoruba

- *The surface of the water is beautiful, but it is no good to sleep on.*
  Ghana

- *If there is character, ugliness becomes beauty; if there is none, beauty becomes ugliness.*
  Nigeria

- *You are beautiful, but learn to work, for you cannot eat your beauty.*
  Congo

- *The one who loves an unsightly person is the one who makes him beautiful.*
  Uganda

- *Having beauty doesn't mean understanding the perseverance of marriage.*
  Africa

- *You are beautiful because of your possessions.*
  Baguirmi (Chad)

- *Every woman is beautiful until she speaks.*
  Zimbabwe

- *Three things cause sorrow to flee; water, green trees, and a beautiful face.*
  Morocco

- *A beautiful thing is never perfect.*
  Egypt

- *Patience is the mother of a beautiful child.*
  Bantu

- *There is no beauty but the beauty of action.*
  Morocco

- *Judge not your beauty by the number of people who look at you, but rather by the number of people who smile at you.*
  Africa

- *Pretty face and fine clothes do not make character.*
  Congo

- *Youth is beauty, even in cattle.*
  Egypt

- *A pretty basket does not prevent worries.*
  Congo

- *It's those ugly caterpillars that turn into beautiful butterflies after seasons.*
   Africa

- *The most beautiful fig may contain a worm.*
   Zulu

- *It is only a stupid cow that rejoices at the prospect of being taken to a beautiful abattoir.*
   Africa

- *A woman who pursues a man for sex loses her spiritual beauty.*
   Africa

- *A chicken with beautiful plumage does not sit in a corner.*
   Africa

- *The cook does not have to be a beautiful woman.*
   Shona

- *Beautiful words don't put porridge in the pot.*
   Botswana

- *She is beautiful. She has love and understands. She respects herself and others. Everyone likes, loves, and honors her. She is a goddess.*
   Africa

- *There is always a winner even in a monkey's beauty contest.*
  Africa

- *Dress up a stick and it'll be a beautiful bride.*
  Egypt

- *An ugly child of your own is more to you than a beautiful one belonging to your neighbor.*
  Uganda

- *Even the colors of a chameleon are for survival not beauty.*
  Africa

- *Beautiful discourse is rarer than emeralds. Yet it can be found among the servant girls at the grindstones.*
  Egypt

- *When a once beautiful piece of cloth has turned into rags, no one remembers that it was woven by Ukwa master weavers.*
  Igbo

- *A woman's polite devotion is her greatest beauty.*
  Africa

- *There are many colorful flowers on the path of life, but the prettiest have the sharpest thorns.*
  Africa

- *He who marries a beauty marries trouble.*
  Nigeria

- *Despite the beauty of the moon, sun and the stars, the sky also has a threatening thunder and striking lightening.*
  Africa

- *Getting only a beautiful woman is like planting a vine on the roadside. everyone feeds on it.*
  Africa

- *Greatness and beauty do not belong to the gods alone.*
  Nigeria

- *Roosters' tail feathers: pretty but always behind.*
  Malagasy

- *Beauty is not sold and eaten.*
  Nigeria

- *She is like a road: pretty, but crooked.*
  Cameroon

- *Why they like an ugly person takes long for a beautiful person to know.*
    Africa

- *If you find "Miss This Year" beautiful, then you'll find "Miss Next Year" even more so.*
    Nigeria

- *The beauty of a woman becomes useless if there is no one to admire it.*
    Africa

chapter notes:

Chapter 10

African Proverbs on Love and Marriage

When Africans fall in love, they tend to become poetic; they are likely too shy to express their feelings. The shyness is due to the fear of rejection or cultural norm. Africans are confused with what comes first: love or marriage, chicken or egg. Elders advise that you don't fall in love with someone you barely know; you are most likely to be infatuated and just want to have sex. They advise to get married first and live together to test if you love each other.

I don't know why love is associated with falling. It is not African to fall in love; it is but to rise in love. Being in love means that you have the power of two within one. Being in love means that you take care of each other, understand each other's feelings, respect each other, and even sacrifice your life for the other.

Africans can get married traditionally with an arranged style of marriage or by searching for the right one themselves. Marriage should be blessed by elders and acknowledged by spiritual leaders. Special ceremonies are performed with music and dance while invited guests are feasting. Married couples have a higher status and respect than singles. They are blessed with grace and children.

Married couples are to abide by cultural and customary laws that make it difficult to get divorced. African couples tend to stay married for a long time. The divorce rate in America is higher because the couples don't know if they are really in love. People are easily divorced because they don't involve elders and respected family members for conflict resolution. Americans tend to divorce because their individual visions and aspirations are different, and couples fail to be true friends.

Here you can see some proverbs about love and marriage.

- *He who loves the vase loves also what is inside.*
  Africa

- *It's much easier to fall in love than to stay in love.*
  Africa

- *Coffee and love taste best when hot.*
  Ethiopia

- *Where there is love there is no darkness.*
  Burundi

- *If you are ugly you must either learn to dance or make love.*
  Zimbabwe

- *Pretend you are dead, and you will see who really loves you.*
  Africa

- *To love the king is not bad, but a king who loves you is better.*
  Wolof

- *A happy man marries the girl he loves, but a happier man loves the girl he marries.*
  Africa

- *If you marry a monkey for his wealth, the money goes, and the monkey remains as is.*
  Egypt

- *Love never gets lost; it's only kept.*
  Africa

- *Never marry a woman who has bigger feet than you.*
  Mozambique

- *One thread for the needle, one love for the heart.*
  Sudan

- *Love has to be shown by deeds not words.*
  Swahili

- *Love is a despot who spares no one.*
  Namibia

- *Marriage is like a groundnut; you have to crack it to see what is inside.*
  Ghana

chapter notes:

Chapter 11

African Proverbs on Patience

Patience is characterized by anticipating and waiting for a result with conscious self-control. People who are patient are mostly winners at the end, as long as they stay focused. There is no patience without hope, because one has to get spiritual assurance that what they need will be fulfilled. Patience is a quality of a person; but not everyone has it.

Patient people are respected by their friends and neighbors; they are the ones whom other people come and look for when they need advice. Patience could have a genetic component because the children of patient people tend to inherit that behavior.

Some people don't get what they want or need within a certain time frame and they lose patience and give up.

Africans learned patience from nature, such as in the relationship between prey and predators. Animals don't just run after their prey, they usually are patient until it is easier to attack.

The length of time a woman bears a child is another way of explaining patience. The time it takes for an elder to climb a mountain is characterized by patience. The time people wait until an oppressing government is overthrown or gone shows patience.

The time one needs to find the truth, or the time it takes when someone is lining up to get a turn are examples of patience.

The younger generation is mostly blamed for a lack of patience in African society. They are always advised not to rush to make decisions. They are always advised to reconsider their actions or inactions.

Americans are usually patient; they don't rush to make decisions based on emotions. However, I see that younger Americans lack patience and suffer the consequences. They can learn from Africans by holding onto their emotions and being careful with their actions.

Here are some words of wisdom related to patience.

- *Patience is the key which solves all problems.*
  Sudan

- *Hurry, hurry has no blessings.*
  Swahili

- *Patience is the mother of a beautiful child.*
  Bantu

- *To run is not necessarily to arrive.*
  Swahili

- *Patience can cook a stone.*
  Africa

- *A patient man will eat ripe fruit.*
    Africa

- *At the bottom of patience, one finds heaven.*
    Africa

- *A patient person never misses a thing.*
    Swahili

- *Patience puts a crown on the head.*
    Uganda

- *Patience attracts happiness; it brings near that which is far.*
    Swahili

- *Always being in a hurry does not prevent death; neither does going slowly prevent living.*
    Ibo

- *However long the night, the dawn will break.*
    Africa

chapter notes:

Chapter 12

African Proverbs on Food

Food has more value than meeting nutritional needs or filling the belly. It brings family to a table together. People invite each other, share their meals, and have conversations over food. Food is a means of forming unity and prosperity.

Food is celebrated in Africa. We prepare special meals for marriages, funerals, births, and religious and cultural celebrations. We offer it to God, make peace with our enemies, and celebrate our independence with food.

It is difficult to mention food without women, who work so hard every day to prepare it. Food is something you miss if you leave your home for various reasons. Mothers and grandmothers are the super chefs who make and store food responsibly. We have various types of dishes, and a certain way of cooking. We use various types of animal products and plant resources to prepare food. Food can help heal the wound and mend the broken spirit, too.

Here are some proverbs related to food.

- *As porridge benefits those who heat and eat it, so does a child benefit those that rear it.*
  Amhara (Ethiopia)

- *The forest not only hides man's enemies, but it's full of man's medicine, healing power, and food.*
  Africa

- *One person is a thin porridge; two or three people are a lump of ugali.*
  Kuria (Tanzania)

- *The man who counts the bits of food he swallows is never satisfied.*
  African

- *Wine, women and food give gladness to the heart.*
  Ancient Egypt

- *The food that is in the mouth is not yet in the belly.*
  Kikuyu

- *You cannot work for food when there is no food for work.*
  Africa

- *The chicken that digs for food will not sleep hungry.*
  Bayombe

- *He who eats another man's food will have his own food eaten by others.*
  Swahili

- *Food gained by fraud tastes sweet to a man, but he ends up with gravel in his mouth.*
  Africa

- *No partridge scratches the ground in search of food for another.*
  Xhosa

- *The grasshopper which is always near its mother eats the best food.*
  Ghana

- *Don't take another mouthful before you have swallowed what is in your mouth.*
  Malagasy

- *Rich people sometimes eat bad food.*
  Kikuyu

- *The impotent man does not eat spicy foods.*
  Congo

- *You should know what's being cooked in the kitchen otherwise you might eat a forbidden food.*
  Africa

- *When the leg does not walk, the stomach does not eat.*
  Mongo (Congo)

- *A healthy person who begs for food is an insult to a generous farmer.*
  Ghana

- *One spoon of soup in need has more value than a pot of soup when we have an abundance of food.*
  Angola

- *Cooked food is not sold for goats.*
  Kikuyu

- *The mouth is stupid. After eating, it forgets who gave it the food.*
  Africa

- *A dog knows the places he is thrown food.*
  Acholi

- *One who eats alone cannot discuss the taste of the food with others.*
  Africa

- *Words are sweet, but they never take the place of food.*
  Ibo

- *The man who has bread to eat does not appreciate the severity of a famine.*
  Yoruba

- *He who doesn't clean his mouth before breakfast always complains that the food is sour.*
  Africa

- *The hyena with a cub does not consume all the available food.*
  Akamba

- *When the food is cooked there is no need to wait before eating it.*
  Kikuyu

- *What one won't eat by itself, one will eat when mixed with other food.*
  Bantu & Lamba

- *Man is like a pepper. Till you have chewed it you do not know how hot it is.*
  Hausa (Chad)

- *No one gets a mouthful of food by picking between another person's teeth.*
  Igbo

- *It is not the cook's fault when the cassava turns out to be hard and tasteless.*
  Ewe

- *A spider's cobweb isn't only its sleeping spring but also its food trap.*
  Africa

- *A housewife who complains that there is not enough foodstuff in the market should remember that if her husband adds to what is already available, there would be more for everyone.*
  Nigeria

- *If you watch your pot, your food will not burn.*
  Mauritania, Nigeria, and Niger

- *Those who are at one regarding food are at one in life.*
  Malawi

- *Fine words do not produce food.*
  Nigeria

- *Even the best cooking pot will not produce food.*
  Africa

- *If I could see your face, I would not need food.*
  Amhara

- *If you find no fish, you have to eat bread.*
  Ghana

- *War is not porridge.*
  Gikuyu

- *The best of mankind is a farmer; the best food is fruit.*
  Ethiopia

- *Slowly, slowly, porridge goes into the gourd.*
  Kuria (Kenya & Tanzania)

- *One shares food not words.*
  Somali

- *If you are looking for a fly in your food, it means that you are full.*
  South Africa

- *Nature gave us two cheeks instead of one to make it easier to eat hot food.*
  Ghana

- *A patient that can swallow food makes the nurse doubtful.*
  Malagasy

- *If you give bad food to your stomach, it drums for you to dance.*
  Africa

- *A bad cook also has his/her share of the bad food.*
  Africa

- *The forest provides food to the hunter after he is utterly exhausted.*
  Zimbabwe

- *Things are to be tried. An old lady cooked stones and they produced soup.*
  Zimbabwe

- *You cannot tell a hungry child that you gave him food yesterday.*
  Zimbabwe

- *Good music goes with good food.*
  Africa

- *Rich people cook their food in a potsherd.*
  Kikuyu

- *However little food we have, we'll share it even if it's only one locust.*
  Malagasy

- *Water is colorless and tasteless but you can live on it longer than eating food.*
  Africa

- *Eat when the food is ready; speak when the time is right.*
  Ethiopia

- *The food eaten first lasts longest in the stomach.*
  Kikuyu

- *When your luck deserts you, even cold food burns.*
  Zambia

- *Happiness is as good as food.*
  Maasai

- *Good words are food, bad words poison.*
  Malagasy

- *The goat says: "Where there is blood, there is plenty of food."*
  Ghana

- *If you see a man in a gown eating with a man in rags, the food belongs to the latter.*
  Fulani

- *They ate our food and forgot our names.*
  Tunisia

- *An abundance of food at your neighbor's will not satisfy your hunger.*
  Bayaka

- *Food you will not eat you do not boil.*
  Africa

chapter notes:

Chapter 13

Proverbs with Various Meanings

Swahili origins:

- *A chicken's prayer doesn't affect a hawk.*
- *The way a donkey expresses gratitude is by giving someone a bunch of kicks.*
- *An envious person requires no reason to practice envy.*
- *It's always good to save or invest for the future.*
- *Hurry—haste has no blessing.*
- *The water pot presses upon the small circular pad.*
- *Effort will not counter faith.*
- *The hen with baby chicks doesn't swallow the worm.*
- *When elephants fight, the grass gets hurt.*
- *I pointed out to you the stars and all you saw was the tip of my finger.*
- *It is only a male elephant that can save another one from a pit.*

- *A deaf ear is followed by death, and an ear that listens is followed by blessings.*

Yoruba origins:

- *He who throws a stone in the market will hit his relative.*
- *A person who stammers would eventually say "father".*
- *One takes care of one's own: when a bachelor roasts yam, he shares it with his sheep.*
- *When a king's palace burns down, the rebuilt palace is more beautiful.*
- *A child lacks wisdom, and some say that what is important is that the child does not die; what kills more surely than lack of wisdom?*
- *You are given some stew and you add water. you must be wiser than the cook.*
- *One does not enter into the water and then run from the cold.*
- *One does not fight to save another person's head only to have a kite carry one's own away.*
- *One does not use a sword to kill a snail.*
- *One gets bitten by a snake only once.*
- *Whoever sees mucus in the nose of the king is the one who cleans it.*

Zulu origins*:*

- *No sun sets without its histories.*
- *A tree is known by its fruit.*
- *The groin pains in sympathy with the sore.*
- *You are sharp on one side like a knife.*
- *The wrong-headed fool, who refuses counsel, will come to grief.*
- *The lead cow (the one in front) gets whipped the most.*
- *Go and you will find a stone in the road that you can't get over or pass.*
- *Hope does not kill; I shall live and get what I want one day.*

chapter notes:

Chapter 14

Major Religions

Africa is a deeply cultural and highly religious continent. There are so many kinds of belief systems existing in Africa, but the dominant ones are Christianity and Islam. The ratio of the number of Africans as a whole, who are Christians to Muslims is around 50:50 throughout the continent, with different numbers among the 55 countries. African Muslims and Christians live in harmony; they are connected with either the same language or tribe, and they are intertwined as a community.

Writing about African proverbs without mentioning the two major religions makes it incomplete and senseless. Populations in Eastern and Northern Africa such as Eritrea, Ethiopia, Egypt, Sudan, and Somalia were among the first to accept and embrace either or both of the two religions before the Middle East. That shows African elders are open minded and wise individuals. Proverbs in the Qur'an and the Bible are subject to interpretation, based on a person's understanding and revelations.

Africans mostly depend on religious scholars, priests, pastors, and sheiks to learn and follow the word of God/Allah.

Africans respect each other and live in harmony, because they have a respect for the creator. They have deeply rooted connections with the Middle East, from where the two major religions originated. The Africans' respect for authority is mostly shaped by religion and the fear of God. The religious celebrations, customs, and rituals are very colorful and have deep meaning.

It is difficult to deny the western influence using religion as a tool. There is a famous quote from Kenya's founder and first president Jomo Kenyatta, who said, "When the missionaries arrived, the Africans had the land and the missionaries had the Bible. They taught us how to pray with our eyes closed. When we opened them, they had the land and we had the Bible."

Africans learned a lot from the past. Their advice to America is to not accept anything just because it sounds convincing. If it is too good to be true, then it may be wrong. The Africans' advice for questioning authority is to question your thought, question your belief, question your leaders, and question your mentors. Find out who you can believe or not and carefully be open and curious.

Religion and science are not two sides of a coin; we need to be open and explore. I've observed that many individuals who live in the west believe that science is a final determinant. There are also many people who say that the only wisdom is through religion. I call both of those beliefs unilateral.

Unilateral wisdom will lead to cognition instability, as it is manifested by grandiosity. It brings confusion and conspiracies that affect the lives of people who are not aware such as: Is global warming real? Are UFO's among us? Are we already ruled by the 666? Did rupture happen? Are we really ruled by a shadow government? Is our food organic and natural? Can we create a hybrid life? What is behind chemtrails? Did we find the magic bullet (a cure to any pathogen or cancer) yet?

Therefore, in order to keep our sanity, we need to stop denying God and start exploring. In order to fulfill our spiritual needs, we need to be open-minded and yearn for the truth. People have followed God for a reason; we have a purpose and a destiny. Our existence is a miracle and we need to value our lives and beyond them.

Denying God is not the answer. We have to open our minds, talk to people, and visit Africa or talk to elders from Africa. Read the literature and seek the wisdom. There is a lot we can learn from Christianity and Islam. At the least, we can learn how to be polite and empathetic. Therefore, I included proverbs which Africans use from the Bible and Qur'an that helped guide them for generations.

Below are some proverbs from the Bible and Qur'an that can help change our perspective.

Proverb Bible Verses About Wisdom

Job 12:12
Wisdom belongs to the aged and understanding to the old. (NLT)

Job 28:28

Behold, the fear of the Lord, that is wisdom, and to depart from evil is understanding. (NKJV)

Psalm 37:30

The godly offer good counsel; they teach right from wrong. (NLT)

Psalm 107:43

Whoever is wise, let him heed these things and consider the great love of the LORD. (NIV)

Psalm 111:10

The fear of the LORD is the beginning of wisdom; all who follow his precepts have good understanding. To him belongs eternal praise. (NIV)

Proverbs 1:7

Fear of the Lord is the foundation of true knowledge, but fools despise wisdom and discipline. (NLT)

Proverbs 3:7

Do not be wise in your own eyes; fear the LORD and shun evil. (NIV)

Proverbs 4:6-7

Do not forsake wisdom, and she will protect you; love her, and she will watch over you. Wisdom is supreme; therefore, get wisdom. Though it cost all you have, get understanding.(NIV)

Proverbs 10:13

Wisdom is found on the lips of him who has understanding, but a rod is for the back of him who is devoid of understanding. (NKJV)

Proverbs 10:19

When words are many, sin is not absent, but he who holds his tongue is wise. (NIV)

Proverbs 11:2

When pride comes, then comes disgrace, but with humility comes wisdom.(NIV)

Proverbs 11:30

The fruit of the righteous is a tree of life, and he who wins souls is wise. (NIV)

Proverbs 12:18

Reckless words pierce like a sword, but the tongue of the wise brings healing. (NIV)

Proverbs 13:1

A wise son heeds his father's instruction, but a mocker does not listen to rebuke. (NIV)

Proverbs 13:10

Pride only breeds quarrels, but wisdom is found in those who take advice. (NIV)

Proverbs 14:1
The wise woman builds her house, but with her own hands the foolish one tears hers down. (NIV)

Proverbs 14:6
The mocker seeks wisdom and finds none, but knowledge comes easily to the discerning. (NIV)

Proverbs 14:8
The wisdom of the prudent is to give thought to their ways, but the folly of fools is deception. (NIV)

Proverbs 14:33
Wisdom rests in the heart of him who has understanding, but what is in the heart of fools is made known. (NKJV)

Proverbs 15:24
The path of life leads upward for the wise to keep him from going down to the grave. (NIV)

Proverbs 15:31
He who listens to a life-giving rebuke will be at home among the wise. (NIV)

Proverbs 16:16
How much better to get wisdom than gold, to choose understanding rather than silver! (NIV)

Proverbs 17:24

A discerning man keeps wisdom in view, but a fool's eyes wander to the ends of the earth.(NIV)

Proverbs 18:4

The words of a man's mouth are deep waters, but the fountain of wisdom is a bubbling brook. (NIV)

Proverbs 19:11

Sensible people control their temper; they earn respect by overlooking wrongs. (NLT)

Proverbs 19:20

Listen to advice and accept instruction, and in the end you will be wise. (NIV)

Proverbs 20:1

Wine is a mocker and beer a brawler; whoever is led astray by them is not wise. (NIV)

Proverbs 24:14

Know also that wisdom is sweet to your soul; if you find it, there is a future hope for you, and your hope will not be cut off. (NIV)

Proverbs 29:11

A fool gives full vent to his anger, but a wise man keeps himself under control. (NIV)

Proverbs 29:15

To discipline a child produces wisdom, but a mother is disgraced by an undisciplined child. (NLT)

Ecclesiastes 2:13

I thought, "Wisdom is better than foolishness, just as light is better than darkness." (NLT)

Ecclesiastes 2:26

To the man who pleases him, God gives wisdom, knowledge and happiness, but to the sinner he gives the task of gathering and storing up wealth to hand it over to the one who pleases God. (NIV)

Ecclesiastes 7:12

For wisdom is a defense as money is a defense, but the excellence of knowledge is that wisdom gives life to those who have it. (NKJV)

Ecclesiastes 8:1

Wisdom brightens a man's face and changes its hard appearance. (NIV)

Ecclesiastes 10:2

The heart of the wise inclines to the right, but the heart of the fool to the left. (NIV)

1 Corinthians 1:18

For the message of the cross is foolishness to those who

are perishing, but to us who are being saved it is the power of God. (NIV)

1 Corinthians 1:19-21
For it is written, "I will destroy the wisdom of the wise, and the cleverness of the clever I will set aside." Where is the wise man? Where is the scribe? Where is the debater of this age? Has not God made foolish the wisdom of the world? For since in the wisdom of God the world through its wisdom did not come to know God, God was well-pleased through the foolishness of the message preached to save those who believe. (NASB)

1 Corinthians 1:25
For the foolishness of God is wiser than man's wisdom, and the weakness of God is stronger than man's strength. (NIV)

1 Corinthians 1:30
It is because of him that you are in Christ Jesus, who has become for us wisdom from God—that is, our righteousness, holiness and redemption. (NIV)

Colossians 2:2-3
My purpose is that they may be encouraged in heart and united in love, so that they may have the full riches of complete understanding, in order that they may know the mystery of God, namely, Christ, in

whom are hidden all the treasures of wisdom and knowledge. (NIV)

James 1:5
If any of you lacks wisdom, he should ask God, who gives generously to all without finding fault, and it will be given to him. (NIV)

James 3:17
But the wisdom that comes from heaven is first of all pure; then peace-loving, considerate, submissive, full of mercy and good fruit, impartial and sincere. (NIV)

Words of Wisdom from the Qur'an

- *Respect and honor all human beings irrespective of their religion, color, race, sex, language, status, property, birth, profession/job and so on. [17/70]*

- *Talk straight, to the point, without any ambiguity or deception. [33/70]*

- *Choose best words to speak and say them in the best possible way. [17/53, 2/83]*

- *Do not shout. Speak politely keeping your voice low. [31/19]*

- *Always speak the truth. Shun words that are deceitful and ostentatious. [22/30]*

- *Do not confound truth with falsehood. [2/42]*

- *Say with your mouth what is in your heart. [3/167]*

- *Speak in a civilized manner in a language that is recognized by the society and is commonly used. [4/5]*

- *When you voice an opinion, be just, even if it is against a relative. [6/152]*

- *Do not be a bragging boaster. [31/18]*

- *Do not talk, listen or do anything vain. [23/3, 28/55]*

- *Do not participate in any paltry. If you pass near a futile play, then pass by with dignity. [25/72]*

- *Do not verge upon any immodesty or lewdness whether surreptitious or overt. [6/151]*

- *If, unintentionally, any misconduct occurs by you, then correct yourself expeditiously. [3/134]*

- *Do not be contemptuous or arrogant with people. [31/18]*

- *Do not walk haughtily or with conceit. [17/37, 31/18]*

- *Be moderate in thy pace. [31/19]*

- *Walk with humility and sedateness. [25/63]*

- *Keep your gazes lowered devoid of any lecherous leers and salacious stares. [24/30-31, 40/19]*

- *If you do not have complete knowledge about anything, better keep your mouth shut. You might think that speaking about something without full knowledge is a trivial matter. But it might have grave consequences. [24/15-16]*

- *When you hear something malicious about someone, keep a favorable view about him/her until you attain full knowledge about the matter. Consider others innocent until they are proven guilty with solid and truthful evidence. [24/12-13]*

- *Ascertain the truth of any news, lest you smite someone in ignorance and afterwards repent of what you did. [49/6]*

- *Do not follow blindly any information of which you have no direct knowledge. (Using your faculties of perception and conception) you must verify it for yourself. In the Court of your Lord, you will be held accountable for your hearing, sight, and the faculty of reasoning. [17/36]*

- *Never think that you have reached the final stage of knowledge and nobody knows more than yourself. Remember! Above everyone endowed with knowledge is another endowed with more knowledge [12/76]. Even the Prophet [p.b.u.h.] was asked to keep praying, "O My sustainer! Advance me in knowledge." [20:114]*

- *The believers are but a single Brotherhood. Live like members of one family, brothers and sisters unto one another. [49/10]*

- *Do not make mockery of others or ridicule others. [49/11]*

- *Do not defame others. [49/11]*

- *Do not insult others by nicknames. [49/11]*

- *Avoid suspicion and guesswork. Suspicion and guesswork might deplete your communal energy. [49/12]*

- *Spy not upon one another. [49/12]*

- *Do not backbite one another. [49/12]*

- *When you meet each other, offer good wishes and blessings for safety. One who conveys to you a message of safety and security and also when a courteous greeting is offered to you, meet it with a greeting still more courteous or (at least) of equal courtesy. [4/86]*

- *When you enter your own home or the home of somebody else, compliment the inmates. [24/61]*

- *Do not enter houses other than your own until you have sought permission; and then greet the inmates and wish them a life of blessing, purity and pleasure. [24/27]*

- *Treat kindly "Your parents", Relatives, "The orphans", And those who have been left alone in the society. [4/36]*

- *Take care of "The needy", "The disabled", "Those whose hard-earned income is insufficient to meet their needs", And "those whose businesses have stalled" And those who have lost their jobs. [4/36]*

- *Treat kindly "Your related neighbors, and unrelated neighbors", companions by your side in public gatherings or public transportation. [4/36]*

- *Be generous to the needy wayfarer, the homeless son of the street, and the one who reaches you in a destitute condition. [4/36]*

- *Be nice to people who work under your care. [4/36]*

- *Do not follow up what you have given to others to afflict them with reminders of your generosity. [2/262].*

- *Do not expect a return for your good behavior, not even thanks. [76/9]*

- *Cooperate with one another in good deeds and do not cooperate with others in evil and bad matters. [5/2]*

- *Do not try to impress people on account of self-proclaimed virtues. [53/32]*

- *You should enjoin right conduct on others but mend your own ways first. Actions speak louder than words. You must first practice good deeds yourself, then preach. [2/44]*

- *Correct yourself and your families first before trying to correct others. [66/6]*

- *Pardon gracefully if anyone among you who commits a bad deed out of ignorance, and then repents and amends. [6/54, 3/134]*

- *Divert and sublimate your anger and potentially virulent emotions to creative energy and become a source of tranquility and comfort to people. [3/134]*

- *Call people to the Way of your Lord with wisdom and beautiful exhortation. Reason with them most decently. [16/125]*

- *Leave to themselves those who do not give any importance to the Divine code and have adopted and consider it as mere play and amusement. [6/70]*

- *Sit not in the company of those who ridicule Divine Law unless they engage in some other conversation. [4/140]*

- *Do not be jealous of those who are blessed. [4/54]*

- *In your collective life, make rooms for others. [58/11]*

- *When invited to dine, go at the appointed time. Do not arrive too early to wait for the preparation of meal or linger after eating to engage in bootless babble. Such things may cause inconvenience to the host. [33/53]*

- *Eat and drink [what is lawful] in moderation. [7/31]*

- *Do not squander your wealth senselessly. [17/26]*

- *Fulfill your promises and commitment. [17/34]*

- *Keep yourself clean, pure. [9/108, 4/43, 5/6]*

- *Dress-up in agreeable attire and adorn yourself with exquisite character from inside out. [7/26]*

- *Seek your provision only by fair endeavor. [29/17, 2/188]*

- *Do not devour the wealth and property of others unjustly, nor bribe the officials or the judges to deprive others of their possessions. [2/188]*

Proverbs from Eritrea,
my original home

- *If an enemy learns your dance, he/she dances it the crooked way.*

- *He who pursues a chicken often falls but the chicken has to continue running.*

- *An owl farted and demanded to be praised by his kinsmen; they mocked him that it is not right to dance to an abomination.*

- *If you hear a mad man talking, wait for a minute and you will soon hear what makes people think he is mad.*

- *An old man who by himself carries one load on the head and another in his hand, must have played away his youth.*

- *If one overeats, he will either throw up or swell up.*

- *Tomorrow is pregnant and no-one knows what she will give birth to.*

- *A fly that doesn't listen to advice usually follows the corpse into the grave.*

- *When you throw a stone at God, it lands right on top of your head.*

- *Dreamers remember their dreams when they are in trouble.*

- *What an old man can see while seated a young man cannot see standing.*

- *Two trees planted together cannot avoid brushing against each other.*

- *When a road is good, it is used a second time.*

- *A fool is a wise man's ladder.*

- *A termite grows up in dry wood, and yet comes to maturity.*

- *The one chased away with a club comes back, but the one chased away with reason does not.*

- *The reason people stab behind you is because you are ahead of them.*

- *I'm still patient until patience gets tired of me.*

- *Aid is like a pill that numbs the pain, if you take it too often you get addicted.*

- *The camel keeps on marching, while the dogs keep on barking!*

chapter notes:

Chapter 15

For Health Care Providers and Others

This study is not about the quality of the proverbs. It is not about measuring IQ or cognitive ability of clients. It is a tool to assess how individuals interact with others: how free they are to express their feelings, how they control their emotions and abide by common laws, and how well you think they will interact with others when they return to the larger community.

When using these proverbs, please be kind and remain free of judgment. Respect the autonomy of the client and be truthful, accurate, and just when making your assessment.

Clients with lots of trauma are vulnerable, and they often view your moves and attentions with increased caution. What you tell them could be life-changing in a positive way or it could cause unintended consequences. What they say in a group setting could incite another member of the group. Don't forget to keep yourself and your clients safe from any danger.

While intended to help people with addictions and social problems who are housed within hospitals, rehab facilities, or pre-release facilities like Walden House, Afro-therapy can be utilized in any kind of behavioral health private or group therapy situation.

In addition, it can also be used beyond the role of assessment in that specific field of healthcare. What if all physicians and nurses were able to use this method to determine a client's ability to communicate, in general, prior to charting their medical histories? Aren't histories sometimes taken incorrectly because of a client's age, way of speaking, disorientation, or fear, etc.? One brief discussion using a simple and positive proverb might put the client at ease or alert the provider to the client's state of mind from the onset of the interview.

chapter notes:

Chapter 16

Other Uses for African Proverbs

The use of African proverbs can also be applied outside of the healthcare field. This is a tool that can be adapted and utilized by any group with common goals.

It can help teachers in any school (at any level) to find common ground to tackle problems together, and it can be used in a number of classrooms for many purposes. Students can interact using these proverbs to identify their preferred peer groups.

It can help the management and employees of any business or organization (be it for profit or non-profit) to resolve conflicts, as a part of job trainings, or even as an activity during presentations at conferences. Executives of organizations can become aware of issues when employees are too shy to talk about them for fear of consequences from their immediate bosses and supervisors. Corporations can use these proverbs to assess how their employees interact with each other and to make sure they are manifesting a friendly culture.

Political party leaders can assess their teams to see if they are truly engaging with their peers or faking it. They surely could use African proverbs to reflect upon their own beliefs and morals, as well as their styles of leadership.

This simple tool can help clubs, such as the YMCA, the Boys and Girls Clubs, or can be used with sports groups (professional or non-professional).

It can be applied in training at any level, for any branch of the military.

Also, it can be helpful for improving communication with family or friends. Parents can interact with their children and create conversations in an environment where they or their children can express their feelings. Parents who are at odds with children who are not open will be helped in their understanding of what their children are going through, so that they can provide help to them. Parents can also use these proverbs to start difficult conversations about sex, reproductive health, abuse, bullying, and harassment.

And, what about using these proverbs for entertainment— as a game during a party or for discussion at other social or religious gatherings? I believe there are many more uses of this tool just waiting to be discovered.

chapter notes:

Chapter 17

What This Study Means to Me

I was inspired by my ancestors, who were capable of changing African lives for the many generations that followed. I would like to praise my elders who created these proverbs and thank my African brothers and sisters, who transferred them to the next generations and documented them. In Africa, they are still widely used during conversations, interactions, and at gatherings. The proverbs have inspired me, as well. I apply them in my own life, especially when I need guidance.

The real beauty of these proverbs is that they can be used in any sector or medium, with little to no cost for the groups participating in conversations!

These proverbs are owned by the public and can be found on the internet for free.

My first objective in writing this was to introduce a way in which these proverbs could specifically benefit the healthcare community in the United States, as well as the American society and other world societies, in general.

My secondary objective was to encourage Americans to claim their affiliation with Africa and to interact with African elders and societies when they go there, or when they meet Africans in the United States. I would like to invite Americans to visit Africa and study what it and its people are all about.

Africa is the second largest continent and it is rich with natural resources, including its people. The population of Africa is diversified with lots of tribes, culture, and extraordinarily beautiful costumes. Africa is not just a jungle. It does have amazing wildlife that live in their natural habitats; but it also has beautiful cities with technologies that have contributed to the betterment of the world for centuries. Africa is a continent where ancient civilizations are found. The African people are beautiful in mind and heart and are remarkable for being true friends.

People may think there are lots of diseases and wars in Africa, but Europe fought more devastating wars than their African counterparts; and most of the problems Africa inherited are due to colonization.

I am proud of being an African. I have explored the wealth of wisdom my ancestors had, and I know that their overlooked contributions can potentially transform lives for the better in America and all over the world. Once again, I thank my ancestors for their wisdom and their teachings. I hope that by sharing this simple but powerful method with you that I, too, have made a contribution that will transform your life.

chapter notes:

Book 2

"Corporationalism":
The End of Ideologies

Chapter 1

Social Classifications

Societies are categorized in four levels based on income. They are: high income, middle income, low income, and poverty. It is not news to reveal that this division started with our ancestors millions of years ago.

Human societies were hunter-gatherers in the beginning. They would keep migrating until they found a place that gave them meals in abundance. They would gather, socialize, and perform rituals.

They talked about ways to save food. They debated about ways to keep themselves safe from dangerous animals and difficult landscapes or environments. They created various ways to gather and secure their meals. Thoughts and opinions regarding ways to adapt and thrive started during those times. People who ate enough only had the chance to communicate. Those who did not gather enough food did not have enough time to enhance their ways of collecting. They only had time to fill their bellies; they didn't have time to be creative.

People started to raise animals they had previously hunted. The introduction of domestication changed their way of life. In order to domesticate, people have to settle. Settlements are one of the preconditions to maintaining safety. Storage of food is another method achieved as an outcome of settlement.

Forming settlements led to a more organized way of life. Family structures composed of elders, warriors, women, and shamans were formed. This organization of people led to the accumulation of wealth. While some societies worked hard, others brutally looted instead. This probably was the beginning of recognized class differences, based on what they gathered, owned, or stole.

Classes are mostly formed based on groups with identical interests. Intragroup class differences would not happen with relatively smaller members of families or clans in an egalitarian society.

The introduction of agriculture in ancient Egypt using cattle changed the wealth level of societies. This helped people to settle adjacent to rivers or other water sources. After people gathered, they would continue to think about how to make their agriculture efficient and effective with less man power, energy, and time. Thought and reasoning increased efficiency. Using thought, people invented tools and, as a result, they were able to create more wealth.

People who produced beyond their physiological needs became powerful. With the creation of wealth, categories of societies started to become visible, and the wealth levels became walls or barriers that separated them from one another.

Human societies transformed their lives after they satisfied their basic needs such as, nutritious food, shelter, clothing, and overall health. Once they learned how to fulfill their basic needs, they started to look for self- and environmental consciousness using increased curiosity. They then developed art, science, and entertainment.

No matter how fortunate we are in other areas, if basic needs such as food, shelter, and clothing cost us more than fifty percent of our income, we are considered poor.

According to UNESCO: *Frequently, poverty is defined in either relative or absolute terms. Absolute poverty measures poverty in relation to the amount of money necessary to meet basic needs such as food, clothing, and shelter.*

My father was a technical school graduate in auto mechanics. He worked so hard to fulfill the basic needs of the family. As a family, we depended on him. Therefore, the only thing I was focusing on, as a child, was my education.

I was free to choose and fulfill my destiny. Dreams that healthy people make are expected to be realistic, with the exception of toddlers, who imagine a lot. If there are no outside factors involved, such as natural or manmade hindrances, people tend to maintain the lifestyle they grew up with. This is an indication that generations tend to stay at the same level category of society as their parents do. I maintained and stayed within the category that my father raised me.

Personal self-caused hindrances such us drug use, alcohol abuse, gambling, and wasting of resources with lifestyle choices beyond means or, on the other hand, imposed hindrances such as war, recession, lack of peace and security, illness, and discrimination can be factors that draw us back to the lower level category in the society we live in.

Imposed hindrances, such as recession and conflicts can be a source of wealth for some people. Wealth can be started with or accumulated more by taking advantage of people who lose their category. I can give you a personal example.

My wife and I immigrated to the United States with 20 dollars in our pockets, and we are amazed and feel blessed when we talk about how we got to the level we are at now. We moved to the United States in 2006, when the economy was booming. However, less known to the public was that it was a bubble.

People were spending beyond their means. Corporations and government organizations invested like there was no tomorrow. Some executives of private corporations became so powerful that they were able to direct policies, change governments, and dictate politics. Some used private airplanes to get to work. For the average citizen, it was relatively easier to find and change jobs that allowed them to borrow uncontrollably. I call it American Collective Madness (ACM). ACM started with politicians who relaxed some laws that governed financial institutions. These crooks worked hand in hand with brokers and rent seekers who frequently traveled between Wall Street and Washington, DC.

ACM was contagious; it spread all the way to California toward Silicon Valley, which produced startups that created multi-millionaires overnight. ACM spread to Europe and threatened to bring down the world economy.

Unfortunately, the bubble exploded with a huge bang. A domino effect, with multiple aftershocks, took the explosion beyond the government's control. The bursting of the bubble was felt all over the world. Within three to four years, we witnessed millions of people throughout the country losing their homes, 401k's, and investments.

All investment prices, including home values, plunged. All the phony companies lost their value and insurance companies were unable to cover the loss. Cities, in their entirety, went bankrupt and the deficit went over ten trillion dollars. Some countries nearly lost their independence. Demographics changed, and stable neighborhoods lost their communities.

Fortunately, people who had good credit, but little savings, were able to buy houses for a fraction of their value. My wife and I were fortunate to save enough money for a down payment, and we were able to buy a house. The deal we got would be unthinkable, if it weren't for the recession. Thanks to my wife's ability to realize that we needed to act fast at the right time, we were able to sell the house we had and buy another one right before housing prices went up. This time, we were able to buy a house in a better neighborhood, which helped us to enroll our kids in a better school district.

What comes next is up to us as a family: how we utilize the resources that we have, and how hard we work to maintain our lifestyle.

How do we break the barrier and advance to the next class category? The success of the previous generation is very important in maintaining the next generation's life style. For instance, a high-income family would have enough financial resources to provide their children with advanced education, health care, and financial support to empower them, which helps maintain their lifestyle. However, it is up to the children to maintain the blessings and keep on going. Though, if they break the barrier and do not use the resources they have wisely, they will fall to the lower level of society and have a lower category lifestyle than their parents.

By the same token, children who are raised in an impoverished family need to work harder to break the barrier, because their parents are unable to provide the means to jumpstart their livelihood; they are struggling just to provide their daily physiological needs. That's the reason the poor tend to stay poor and the rich tend to stay rich for generations.

Families need to evolve, because the rule of the game is natural selection. Generally, the next generation should work harder and smarter to maintain their lifestyles, or they risk losing the achievements of the previous generation.

I grew up in a place and time when socialism was considered the best style of leading a nation. One of the propagandas I remember was: "Everyone contributes based on his or her ability, and everyone gets paid what he or she deserves for the work done."

This basically meant that creativity was not rewarded; everyone shared the wealth of the country equally and everyone was equally poor. The politicians at that time set a goal or a vision for a country using various propagandas that sounded impressive but were empty when delivering the people's needs. One was: "Everyone works based on his or her ability, and everyone gets paid the way he or she desires." This is pure communism.

I was born in the mid 70's in Ethiopia, where a military junta ruled and was leading the poor country towards communism, after overthrowing the self-claimed "thousand-year Solomonic monarchy", ruled by the last king, Haile Selassie.

At that time, many students were obsessed with Mao Zedong's red book. The students thought they could achieve their goals when it was declared the end of feudalism led by the king. Homes were confiscated along with land from landlords and given to the public. The self-claimed communists took over private firms. The population was forced to organize into unions, such as urban dwellers, farmers' associations, workers' unions, youth leagues, women's leagues, and so on.

The government limited the people's incomes and outlawed owning capital that exceeded 500,000 Birr (an Ethiopian currency). Everyone became equal. The people felt they owned everything after hearing the propaganda that said they confiscated from the rich and made it available to the poor. The government promised to hire them in more industries without considering the capacity.

The farmers ploughed their land in associations. They received tools and fertilizer free of charge at first, then followed by smaller loans. The country started to be ruled based on campaigns copied from Mao, without considering the culture. There was a slight increase in productivity for a while that made people praise socialism.

Private firms faded away, which caused problems with trade competition. Demands went higher than supplies, which affected innovation. The unintended outcome of socialism was the inability of countries to develop.

The people become equally poor and mass-starved. The vision was to pay everyone according to their needs. However, the goal was unachievable due to imbalances in the economy; that was the reason for the failure of socialism.

My observation of American society is that there is no alternative but capitalism, with some socialism in the mix as a form of social service; and ownership of land, home, and small business is encouraged. The vision is for everyone to live the American dream after achieving ownership.

There are several ways to be an owner in America: complete higher education to make money, get into politics to make money, bid for an office to make money, wait until parents die to inherit money, or involve yourself in illegal drugs, prostitution, theft, or fraud and so on to make money.

Are people living the dream? What was the dream really—just to own a piece of land or a home for which people immerse themselves in huge debt? What happened to the people was that they became self-centered, stressed, impatient, or lacking in family values in order to win the rat race. Americans are great at making money, but poor with spending. They live beyond their means and they borrow beyond their capacity. If they get sick, they pay huge medical bills and drain their hard-earned savings. They have school and credit card debt that they can't afford to pay off.

People see the waste of wealth for which they worked so hard. The problem begins with individual citizens and spreads to the city, state, and federal level. This is another American Collective Madness (ACM).

One of the wastes that worries me is food. I bet if someone conducts a study, they will find that people throw away more than they eat. The other waste is energy. Again, people pay for extra energy that they don't need; forgetting to turn off the light, unwanted use of air-conditioning and heating, driving long distances for unproductive reasons, etc. When it comes to the government, it's things like war spending, maneuvers on deep oceans, supporting the wrong allies, spending on miscalculated policies, loopholes, and corruption, to name a few.

There are lots of wasted resources in the American society that will add to the debt, and citizens will only wake up from their dreams to find they have lost their piece of America, due to excessive debt.

I believe there should be a cap on the foreign debt in relation to China, because it will make us weak when we negotiate trade deals with its government. In addition, outsourcing projects to China poses national security implications, due to economic sabotages related to spying and intellectual, patent, and copyright violations.

chapter notes:

Chapter 2

"Corporationalism" Defined

A corporation is a human or collection of humans and their resources. An "-ism" is a school of thought. Therefore, "corporationalism" is the term I've created to mean: The thought that it's possible for the human socioeconomic development cycle to achieve its ultimate goal when two or more people form an organization with synergy for a common goal. In addition, they need to have non-monetary values that bind them together. They need to have a similar vision for a common goal, or their visions should be in paths that meet at one point in their journeys toward different goals. Parallel paths toward goals cannot satisfy corporationalism, and they lead to the collapse of the organization they formed.

Everything should be ruled in such a way that corporations work. The simplest example of corporationalism is the concept of marriage. Individuals (with different or similar goals) unite with a shared vision. The union is acknowledged by the state and blessed by God. The couples are the board members of their union, with one of them acting as the habitual leader. Marriage fails when the couple's vision follows a parallel path.

Corporationalism can be exercised in small business and in every organization (be it for profit or nonprofit), social services, education, municipalities, the military, the congress, the courts, etc. These organizations are run by individuals with a common vision. Corporations are governed by a board, either elected or based on merit.

In contrast, imperialism is the highest level that capitalism can reach. It is a human socioeconomic cycle where wealth is under a monopoly of a handful of corporations or individuals. At this stage, the handful become the visionaries, and people work to satisfy the vision of the handful. There is a loss of common goal and diminished human development. Social services, social capital, and social justice issues will be in question.

The only thing that links the monopolies and their workers will be money. Workers in an imperialistic society make relatively more money than their capitalist counterparts, due to the cost of living.

Imperialism will be at risk of collapse due to greed by the monopolies, (in today's term, the 1 percent) when governments are fully under their control. Karl Marx would have suggested the oppressed 99 percent will rise and confiscate (nationalize) wealth from the 1 percent and distribute it among themselves, which will lead to the birth of socialism.

There is no country today that has reached an imperialist stage. This issue makes people question Marxism as a phony philosophy, because monopolies are being regulated by the government, and social justice issues are crucial in any form of government on the globe.

Corporationalism is a form of ruling that goes back to a person. Some 400 years ago, the law used to be "the king." The law evolved and became a paper: "We the People", the Constitution of the United States. However, we are now back to corporationalism, the rule of a person. This became certain during the US Supreme Court ruling of *Citizen's United v. Federal Election Commission (FEC)*. This ruling opened a can of worms; it recognized a corporation's political participation as a human right issue.

In 1978, a sharply divided Supreme Court ruled for the first time that corporations have a First Amendment right to spend money on state ballot initiatives. Still, for decades, candidate elections remained free of direct corporate influence under federal law.

"A corporation is a person." There was a lot of outrage on this issue, especially during the 2008 economic downturn that threatened the world order. Currently, both parties nearly agree against the *Citizen's United* ruling, but I don't see anyone trying to change it. There is no limit on the influence of corporations on elections. One of the examples of corporation hegemony is the NRA (National Rifle Association.)

The 150-year-old association with 5 million members single-handedly influenced all campaigns against gun laws and defeated the country's political party that has more members. Nothing stopped the NRA, not even after the public outrage that followed mass shootings at schools in various states.

My personal stand on this is in line with the Citizens United, Supreme Court rule that "A corporation is a person." Anything can be said to challenge this issue; however, no one can deny that corporations are basically made of persons. Therefore, corporations are persons. The only difference is that corporations are not biological beings. They are legal beings, created with certain structure and resource that make their members unite to be stronger in fulfilling their visions and to separate issues of liability from each of them personally.

By default, corporations elect officials, take government contracts, help overthrow governments, and lead religious and tribal institutions. They even help people by becoming relief organizations. Even God is a corporation in my view; it is a leadership of three entities united as one, with a vision of being a source of agape for all humanity, as stated in the Bible in John 3:16.

I am sure people were confused when the founding fathers refused to form an American kingdom but wrote the Constitution instead. People in Europe, and other parts of the world, teased at that time by saying how come people are ruled by a paper?

What seems new here was exercised by the Jews, when Moses delivered the tablet of the Ten Commandments. In contrast to the constitutional rule, which is subjected to amendment as centuries go by, Judeo-Christianity is ruled by tablet-paper with the Ten Commandments transformed to the rule of love and doesn't require amendment as a source of all laws.

However, the rule of government isn't as scientific as the rule of Christianity. In other words, government rule philosophically lags behind religious rule. After 400 years, the law of the Constitution transformed back to a person (a corporation), ever since the Citizens United ruling, putting it at risk for imperialism.

I can provide some examples based on my view. For instance, why are we in endless wars? Corporationalism, as a form of government, outsources to the military industrial complex (MIC). If MIC as a person needed to survive, there should be wars.

The MIC could not have survived if there were no Middle East conflicts, such as Palestine, Israel, Syria, Libya, and Iraq, or other places like Somalia, Afghanistan, and the Ukraine. The United States became an actor, in addition to other superpowers like Russia, France, and Britain in these conflicts, due to our influence ever since World War II.

The Cold War became a chance to develop and mass produce weaponry. The MIC is continuing to make money. The problem is the influence it may cause if longer periods of peace persist, which is a threat to its existence.

There is no war in the world that the United States was not involved in. People are paying a huge price, and as the price tag becomes bigger, so does the corruption. We've heard of money and weapons in the hands of terrorists that they indirectly received from the United States government at various times.

Another example can be the financial sector. Banking and insurance institutions wouldn't survive if there were no term (predatory) loans. Oil corporations cannot survive the cost of spilling, if it wasn't for the regulators, who are indirectly elected by them and their puppets.

Corporations as people evolved to rule the world by making constituencies. They are heavily involved in politics by contributing a lot of money, so that they have their representatives in office. They are known to transfer capital to countries with low taxes and low regulations. They use every loophole to avoid paying their share. This is typical egoistic human behavior.

I am arguing for corporations as a human, because I couldn't find any other alternatives. It is the reality. It is a normal human socioeconomic cycle that was waiting to happen. However, we can manage corporationalism using the parallel method.

chapter notes:

Chapter 3

The Parallel Method

The human struggle should focus against corporate monopoly because it leads to imperialism. Imperialism is inversely proportional to the struggle for social justice. The only way we can fight should be by strengthening our work on social justice.

We, the common people, can line up for support if corporations have a vision that crosses or is in line with our vision of "social justice for all." However, we need to fight them when their vision is parallel to issues of social justice.

We have to stay parallel to monopoly; monopoly is very resourceful, powerful, and hard to regulate because it is tied in with our needs. Imagine what would happen if major oil producers stopped exporting oil. Look at what's happened with pharmaceutical companies; they've increased prices beyond control. As we know, most medications are patented and cannot be produced and supplied by another company. Imagine if the American International Group (AIG) was allowed to fail and the implications to the world financial sector, as a result.

The National Rifle Association (NRA) is one of the corporations that has become a monopoly and follows a parallel path with the commons, when it comes to gun laws. Why can't we establish an inclusive NRA like an organization, one that includes students, parents, teachers, and similar interest groups that advocate for gun laws? The NRA currently controls the conversation around the gun laws because it is an organized corporation. Think of the impact the International Monetary Fund (IMF), and the World Bank has on the world economy.

Therefore, we need to put a cap on corporations, so they won't become monopolies and in order to: keep our oil coming, have medications regulated and priced better, regulate the Internet service providers (because the companies are so powerful that it's difficult to imagine if they merged), and keep our schools safer from gun violence.

chapter notes:

Chapter 4

Order Above—Chaos Below

The idea of above and below doesn't mean heaven and earth, as the way previous philosophers put it. It is a cycle of order and chaos among the hierarchy in various forms of socioeconomic order.

Order began with egalitarian societies who were hunter-gatherers ruled by women, elders and shamans. Women introduced gathering while men mainly hunted. Unfortunately, hunting was risky and the quantity men brought was limited. Therefore, most of the meals were gathered by women.

Women were the core of the economy. Elders oversaw the distribution of meals and they were the keepers of social justice. Shamans were responsible for physical and spiritual healings. This socioeconomic order was an organic and practical order for a longer human history. Order above was maintained with the hierarchy maintaining its responsibility, and social justice was practiced.

The order was in danger when the above could not handle the chaos that came from below.

Societies lived in order until the transition to a slave-based economy. Slave-based economy was a product of the transfer of the rule of women to men, due to the power they accumulated because they had time for thought. The basic needs were handled by women, therefore men went to war with other men to take over resources, instead of hunting. The powerful accumulated wealth and made the war prisoners their slaves. This led to the development of the free economic powerhouse that gave birth to a slave-based socio-economic society.

The cycle cannot be created or imposed by politicians on a country. Evidence for this is the failure of imposed communism, that ended with the collapse of the Soviet Union, Germany, and Czechoslovakia during the Cold War. This cycle can only be evolved by imbalance between order above and chaos below.

A slave-based economy has a hierarchy (above) of men, religious leaders and soldiers, who maintain order by taking over other's riches and increase productivity using slaves. This order would come to an end when the common people left the cities and depended upon the productivity that was based on agriculture. That led to the birth of feudalism.

Feudalism, as a socioeconomic cycle, bases its economy on land. The order above was composed of owners of vast land and tenants who worked on their lands. The owners attracted slaves by promising them a small share of produce (either 90%-10% or 80%-20%, depending on the country). Slaves started to run away from cities and become tenants who ploughed lands and raised farm animals.

They felt relatively free and started to own a small share of the products, which led to the boom in agriculture. Order was maintained for a while. The land owners who became powerful started to send their children to the cities for education and exploration, so that they could contribute to strengthening the feudal system. However, the rich kids who were sent to cities learned to develop industries in the cities by depending on raw materials that came from agriculture. These kids developed industry by decreasing input and maximizing output using machinery. They learned to mass-produce cheese and other dairy products, beer, and bread, instead of selling raw milk and grains that were produced on the farm. And, in order to maximize the scale of productivity, they offered tenants who lived on farms a higher pay and life in the cities. That led to the Industrial Revolution.

The feudal order was destroyed due to the mass migration of tenants looking for work in the cities. Industries flourished, and cities developed and populated. Investments to build infrastructures continued. This led to capitalism, the world order we are in now.

The children of the feudal socioeconomic system became richer than their parents. They developed ideas, art flourished, science and math advanced. Countries formed, and laws were created. The desire to limit liabilities led to the birth of the corporation.

Corporationalism as a socioeconomic cycle flourished and became the order that prevailed against communism and socialism. Corporations exist in various forms. They can be governmental organizations; city, state and federal administrations; nonprofit organizations; religious, educational, or agricultural institutions; the oil and energy sectors; financial institutions; and so on.

The order above is board members, capitalists, religious leaders, university and researchers (philosophers on top), employees and unions, the military and security, farmers, students, and religious worshipers.

The risk at this time, however, is monopoly. Monopoly would lead to imperialism, which threatens the livelihood of the commons. The commons are relatively richer than the tenants who worked under the feudal system.

The commons can only survive when they have guarantees for healthcare, food, security, housing and issues related to energy and the environment. They need to retire peacefully, they need to own homes, and they need to participate in governance.

Social justice is the common vision. However, monopoly (of any form) is a center of gravity, and a reason for resistance. That's my reason for writing this book: so that people are aware and make sure that imperialism doesn't return.

Old Theory

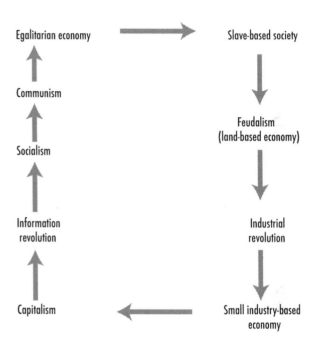

Revised Theory of Society

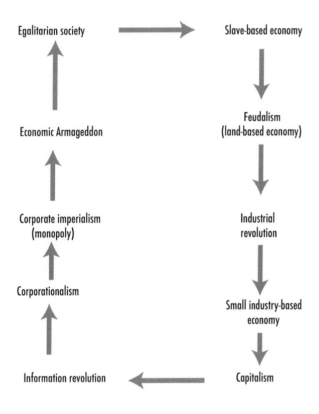

Egalitarian society → Slave-based economy

Slave-based economy → Feudalism (land-based economy)

Feudalism (land-based economy) → Industrial revolution

Industrial revolution → Small industry-based economy

Small industry-based economy → Capitalism

Capitalism → Information revolution

Information revolution → Corporationalism

Corporationalism → Corporate imperialism (monopoly)

Corporate imperialism (monopoly) → Economic Armageddon

Economic Armageddon → Egalitarian society

chapter notes:

Chapter 5

Corporationalism in Developing Countries

It is the new fashion that developing countries have adopted corporationalism in all sectors of their administrations.

These countries are found in Africa, Asia, and Latin America. Most of the countries on these continents have something in common: rich, natural resources such as minerals, oil, vast farming lands, lakes, and rivers that are there only to be admired by their populations who are unable to utilize them. Most of all, they have human resources who live in poverty.

These countries were formed by European colonialists, with a few exceptions. The colonialists exploited their resources and their populations. They divided them, based on religion or clans, in order to exploit them for a long period of time and control rebellion.

It is so fortunate that the United States is the only successful country to emerge better after independence. The only problem for the United States has been the time and resources it took in order to form unity toward the nation's building.

If it wasn't for World War II, I doubt that most countries would be independent. World War II was the fight between superpowers to maintain or change the world order.

The US actually was the sole winner after emerging from a long dormant status since its independence. This was due to the long-awaited national building process after successive wars in order to limit its boarders and solve the main cause of the Civil War. The United States took its rightful place in the world order, as a result of prevailing in World War II.

Now, let's go back to the developing world. Why are most of the people in these countries still living in poverty? Each country has its own history that is associated with problems unique to its geopolitical place in the world. In general, however, it is the social cycle that is responsible for the problems.

As mentioned on the diagram of the socioeconomic cycle, they needed to transform their economy. However, they weren't able to follow the cycle with successive wars and exploitation against colonialism and internal conflicts.

European colonialism caused a significant damage to these societies by exploring and utilizing the natural and human resources that had been inherited from the ancestors of those particular countries.

The colonialists took away resources, shipped populations of the people as slaves, and created divisions that made the natives fight each other. They shipped the resources to the booming industries in Europe and America. They physically took people to work as slaves for their vast agricultural plantations.

The people that were under the rule of the colonies were administered by using the theory of divide and conquer.

They also used religious, tribal and/or geographical differences to their advantage. The divisions created by those colonizers are still responsible for the unrest and destabilization of those countries which continues to hinder the national building process.

The macroeconomics of these countries depend mainly on natural resources instead of finished products, due to the inability to invest in infrastructures and industries. Capital is scarce in these countries and they have not been able to jumpstart their economies on a tangible basis.

Exploiting natural resources created corruption and environmental degradation that led to natural disasters. In order to secure capital, these countries were forced to look for western financial institutions that can only survive using predatory loans.

Here is where the trap began. The countries secured the capital, but the predatory loans skyrocketed for developing industries and building infrastructures. They even allocated their annual budgets with significant rates to be covered by loans.

This habit put them in a cycle that led to payment to only cover the interest, and they put themselves under the grip of western corporations (or so-called developmental partnerships formed by them and the developed countries and their institutions), such as the World Bank and IMF.

The only way they seemed to get relief from their skyrocketed debt was by putting social justice issues on hold and removing services from their citizens. They took more loans by proposing to build huge projects such as railways, land leases (I call it grabs), dams, port and airport expansions, and so on, when both parties knew the projects were white elephants. The loan institutions paid bribes (as a commission) to politicians and heads of state, to get them to sign contracts.

The only way out of the loans they saw was to sell bonds, limit services and security, and let go of public workers, which led to more debt and unhappy societies. Financial institutions required developing countries to adjust their structures from down at the bottom to the hierarchy that extends all the way to the predatory institutions in a corporate structure. They forced the countries to reveal their projects and even had these institutions rewrite their macroeconomic plans. They basically gave up their independence on a silver platter. Unfortunately, ignoring their citizens led them to further poverty, chaos, and unstable governments.

So, who rules the developing countries? What is the way out of the current situation? We need to know the core problem before proposing the solution. The developing countries entered imperialism as a socioeconomic cycle, due to monopolies created by western corporations. As mentioned earlier, imperialism is a system that made corporations or individuals into monopolies that provided services in these countries.

Imperialism keeps draining resources with no limit in sight. The corporations have bigger income than the Gross National Income (GNI) of countries, which makes the countries unable to regulate. Nationalizing, refusing to pay debts, or cutting ties with these corporations would put the countries at risk.

The corporations can conspire and change governments. They can get politicians to impose sanctions or can have these countries physically invaded the way we saw in

Colombia, Somalia, Libya, and Iraq. Therefore, the governments have no choice. In order to continue existing, they must continue to pay these monopolies.

In my view, the only way out is to get out of monopolies (imperialism) and back to corporationalism. Basically, countries should restructure to become corporations. They should work hard to minimize the influence of multinational corporations. They need to work on restoring social justice for their citizens. They should stop forming administrations based on divisions of ethnic or religious lines. They need to look at countries that are high on social justice as role models. Those countries are Scandinavian (Norway, Finland, and Sweden). They need to avoid white elephants and take away power from the politicians who are responsible for negotiating with predator corporations. Instead, they need to involve a board that includes representatives from the people, as well as socioeconomic and patriotic intellectuals. They need to appoint a board of citizens to approve loans, instead of officials such as presidents and prime ministers. They should outlaw any form of commission and make gifts the properties of the states. They should administer within their means and not set budgets they don't have or make investments which have no returns.

chapter notes:

Chapter 6

Corporationalism...The End of Ideologies and Democracy

Corporationalism is involved in all sectors of administrations. It overruled all forms of organized political ideology that was visibly running the show ever since the Soviet Revolution in 1917. By 1999, career politicians lost the game in their field. Corporationalism ended ideological politics and economies.

Since the end of the Cold War in 1991, politicians have pretended to follow either liberal or developmental democracy as an ideological game plan to manage politics. Nothing has been invented, and now there are other names for capitalism and Leninism, respectively.

There is hardly such a thing as liberal or developmental that goes hand-in-hand with democracy. Liberals use the party as a base for getting into office. Then, they team up to use state power to lead the party. On the other hand, developmental democrats collectively lead the state using their party as a powerbase.

Liberals give more power to formal governmental structures, and developmentalists give more power to their party. An example of liberal democracy is the United States, who gives more power to governmental structures, and the parties only help to recruit and bring the elites to power. On the other hand, China, Russia, and most of the former communist countries give the ruling party more power over governmental structures.

Trying to identify the difference in administration feels like separating yin from yang. These structures only hurt the countries, because over-focusing on power struggles among parties will give corporations the chance to interfere in politics. As a result, politicians and law makers will hold onto their vision of trying to impress corporations who fund their campaigns. At the end, they fail to manage corporationalism.

China uses developmental democracy as a system of governance. China, in my opinion, is at risk of collapse due to the system which is prone to corruption and will become the first country to reach imperialism. This will happen as soon as the party-owned corporations turn into monopolies. For this reason, China will fail to maintain social justice, and its huge population will migrate all over the world. China's failure will impact the world economy, in general, and all of the third world countries, in particular, who took out loans and investments in order to work with the party-owned corporations. This is my warning to Chinese policy makers.

Politicians and public servants should consider corporationalism when they work on strategies. They should focus on issues of social justice and close all the loopholes, so that they can avoid any form of monopoly.

Our two main political parties in the United States campaign for their programs in commercial ads. They spend huge amounts of money that they get from corporations and interest groups during elections. However, once the officials are elected, we barely see any difference in administration from their previous rivals, except for their tones. The elected officials are visibly dormant and legislate on a bipartisan line to fulfill both corporate and interest group demands.

One example is the campaign that led to the election of Barack Obama. People elected him because he was academically qualified, could speak well, and utilized the Internet better than his opponents. It seems to be part of the culture in the US that Americans adore underdogs, and they made him their favorite when they realized he was treated unfairly by the birthers.

His main visions were as follows: He wanted to amend the broken healthcare system. He was opposed to the war in the Middle East. He promised to bring our troops home by ending the longest war. He promised to close down Guantanamo. These were some of the visions that helped build and mobilize supporters for his campaign. However, powerful corporations made it nearly impossible to fulfill his campaign promises.

After he was elected, he actually didn't stop the war, even though his tone was against it. He didn't bring back our troops and failed to close Guantanamo. He did accomplish putting an affordable health care plan into action. Even that, however, has been under constant attack and has changed since its passing into law. No doubt, powerful pharmaceutical lobbyists and the American Medical Association (along with other special interest groups) are responsible for this. While the law was meant to help individual citizens, it does not satisfy the collective greed of those corporations and their leaders who oppose it.

Corporations wouldn't allow stopping the war effort. He had no choice but continue to feed the corporations that are tied to the venture of war. President Obama is a person I respect and admire. His "Change and Hope" slogan was his ticket to the office that I once appreciated the most. Unfortunately, however, many of his campaign visions were not allowed to be fulfilled. The citizens of multiple generations made history by electing him as the first black president in this country's 250-year-plus history. Four hundred years ago, in 1619, the arrival of the first black people (in what is now known as America) was documented. Obama left a legacy as one of the most graceful and best speakers the United States has ever produced.

Other presidents have won the favor of this country's citizens by using other techniques. George W. Bush was not a good speaker. His ticket to the office of president was scaring people with terrorism and the "axis of evil" and "with us or against us" labeling. In the last election, Donald Trump scared the people by demonizing immigrants. He continues this tactic today, as a means for securing funding for his "Border Wall."

Members of both parties, but Democrats in particular, make it look like Americans are divided along lines of race more today than at any other time in recent history. On the contrary, I argue that this philosophy is testing the people's intelligence. People are not divided along lines of race. People are not experiencing a "new form of racism" today; they have lived it all their lives.

I don't think Americans are as scared of immigrants as Team Trump wants them to be. Institutional racism didn't create discrimination against women; it's always been there. The election of Donald trump is a result of lack of choice. People were only left to choose between the bad and the worst. They elected the bad.

One of the loopholes of democracy is the voting process itself. We elect officials based on their proposals to implement temporary or permanent fixes to governance. Unfortunately, politicians cannot change the ideals of corporationalism. The only thing they can do is to reposition themselves to assimilate within it. That is the reason why people always feel betrayed and have to wait four more years to see if a better person comes around.

Remember: We, the people, have the power! We need to unite to protect our democracy. One of the achievements of the American people was forming strong labor unions that challenged corporations. Corporationalism retaliated and attacked unions.

The number of unions and their members diminished because workers distanced themselves for fear of losing their jobs, especially after the recession. As a result, corporations paid less for more work and, as a result, money started to flow toward the so-called one percent and widen the income gaps further.

Some of the problems of this time, in my view, are explained as follows. Unions were losing power due to lower membership and their executives' political prostitution with corporations. Employees were forced to give up the struggle and do their best to maintain their jobs. Corporations worked tirelessly to force the workers to refuse to actively participate and pay membership fees. They tried to convince them that unions were useless and outdated. The United States is losing unions and risking the struggle for social justice. As a citizen of this great country, this is a warning for the good people among my fellow countrymen and women.

The other problem concerns the deficit. The political structure is indirectly elected and run by corporations and interest groups. They are responsible for the huge budget deficits in almost all state and local administrations. Corporations are hugely influencing our administrations by disabling the political process. Budgets are allocated with projects that help corporations make more money.

The political parties are in a trap; they are tied up by interest groups. This is the main reason we don't see any tangible difference in successive administrations. Once party officials are in office, all promises made are broken. They actually disappoint people by using scare tactics and distractors such as wars and scandals.

The media is one of the culprits of corporate hegemony. They are either on one side or the other of the corporate interests of oil companies (who need to expand the oil business) and agricultural companies (who are afraid of land and water contamination). The Keystone XL pipeline project is an example of how Fox News and NBC influence views based on their corporate predetermined political opinions.

What we don't hear them say is based on an independent environmental and socioeconomic risk assessment, if beneficial to America. They are only debating on a polarized opinion that keeps the people watching them confused. What I wish to see is for news organizations to voice several opinions. With that type of viewing, the people can choose what is best, instead of taking a stand on one side or the other and dictate politics.

We are in a cycle of a dominant and minority party, one after the other. What is happening is that officials are Democrats or Republicans just to assume office, but do not perform any differently once there. This shows the death of the implementation of political promises and, therefore, political ideologies.

chapter notes:

Chapter 7

Fellow Americans,
We Can Do Better!

The Declaration of Independence was one of the remarkable moments in the history of not only the United States, but also the world. "Life, liberty, and the pursuit of happiness" are the inalienable rights of humans that are given by God. The phrase can be simple or complicated.

The colonists, who ran away from Europe due to religious persecution, starvation, or to look for opportunities in the New World, found themselves ruled again by the British. The unfair taxation and class difference led the people to fight against the British monarchy, so that they could live in liberty and pursue happiness. These people started the republic called The United States of America.

The people didn't seek life, liberty, and the pursuit of happiness to be granted by the government they formed. They tried their best to restrict and put government in check so that it didn't become a burden. It is puzzling to me that these very people, who ran to the new world to pursue happiness, started to deprive others of their rights by owning, buying, selling, and abusing slaves from Africa. Africans were displaced and separated from their lands and tribes to become American properties.

Americans fought for their liberty and the pursuit of happiness, while Africans were deprived of the same rights long after the country was formed.

I remember talking to one fellow who told me that the solution for lasting peace for African Americans is to create their own autonomy within the United States territory. He did not mention where that territory is, though. In my opinion, creating autonomy or forming a new country doesn't guarantee liberty and the happiness a society wants to pursue.

My suggestion for the political solution for oppressed communities to pursue happiness is to think about corporationalism during their struggle. Structure a country based on anything else other than race, religion, ethnicity, gender, or political partition.

A corporation is neither a race nor a religion, ethnicity, or gender. It is a group of humans that work together to turn a shared vision into reality. There should be a path through reconciliation to integrate society. Stop the divisions. All races should work for the American collective cause, instead of divided issues. Racial or community struggles should be inclusive of all its members.

Imagine if Black Lives Matter included white members on its board or if an ultra right, white group chose Hispanics and blacks to be on its board? What if the CIA was led by a Muslim, or the YMCA elected a woman to its board, or the housing authority included a homeless person in its leadership?

It all sounds impossible, but that's probably because these are things that haven't been tried. I am suggesting them because I assume every group perceives they are fighting for a right cause. Jesus managed to be friends with thieves, tax collectors, and prostitutes but did not join the corrupted religious leaders.

My fellow Americans, we need to recheck our social justice systems, schools, social services, housing and prisons that are structured similarly to that of a panopticon, a triangular one-way control system overlooked by corporations. A panopticon lacks transparency by labeling humans. For a panopticon, humans are either plagues, or otherwise. Humans are either good or bad, friends or enemies, etc.

A panopticon would label your child as Attention Deficit Hyperactivity Disorder (ADHD), and you would have to give them medications, or your child would not be allowed to go to public schools. If your child is linked to a petty crime, a lasting destination would be in and out of the prison system for the rest of his or her life. No one hires a perceived criminal, and the only choice left is to commit more crime. This is an endless cycle that steals lives and destroys families.

When the prison cycle is too much to handle, your child will have mental illness or addiction, and then will be transferred to the panopticon hospital system. Your child would be labeled a danger to self or society and declared 51/50, or 52/50 and condemned to the chemical prison cycle. (In

California, these are legal terms used by emergency and police personnel to put people who are attempting to commit suicide or pose a danger to others in a psychiatric clinic.)

Another scenario is that your child may lose health care and social services and end up in the homeless cycle. Once your child loses everything, he or she will end up becoming the face of several nonprofit corporations begging for money.

I only have written what I have observed. We can do better than this. We can spend more money and allocate more resources than any other developed country. Yet, we have a lot of prisoners, mentally ill, and homeless among the people of the western world. How do we pursue happiness when we continue to use the idea of a panopticon? We must do better than this. This is a warning to our people.

chapter notes:

Chapter 8

My Suggestions to the People of the United States of America

As a result of my observations, I would like to point out the following suggestions that we need to consider as a society.

Inclusive organizations are needed when we struggle for the same or similar cause. Unions should include HR managers. Women's organizations should include men. Racial organizations should be open to supporters from other races. Anti-addiction organizations should include addicts.

We need to reach out to corporate executives, so that they join the struggle for social justice. They can play a big role in our communities. They can help with housing, healthcare, social services, and education.

Please be careful with planning your personal or corporate goals. I strongly suggest clearing a path to a goal rather than to chase a goal. Thinking of John the Baptist's "clear the path" will lead you to the goal.

Please refrain from living like ants and grasshoppers; add spirituality to your life.

Question authority but refrain from herd mentality and street justice.

Listen to motivational speeches twice; don't over-focus and don't generalize.

Visit your neighbors; know what they are up to. Know their problems; have coffee with them.

Acknowledge and seek praise. As long as you do good, do not be afraid to tell others.

We have a beautiful country; go take a hike and connect with nature.

We are all the same; a pile of dirt with a sprinkle of energy. Cherish it; do not use it to harm others.

Americans are generous people, but we need to know who we are giving to and what percentage of the money we give goes to the right sources and for the right reasons.

Continue to be patriotic and hold onto your love for country. Respect family values.

Avoid labeling. Do not describe your parents with one word. Parents are not just strict, loving, abusive, immigrants, selfish, or cruel etc. They have a lifetime of experience from which you can learn. They are not just one thing or another. This applies to all people.

Set an example. Don't expect your children to be what you tell them to be; be that person first.

Respect the environment and our natural resources because they belong to no one person, but to all of us.

Be faithful. Be loving and kind to yourself and each other.

Corporations are not enemies. Let's be one of them and change them from the inside out.

Visit an African country at least once in your lifetime.

chapter notes:

Bibliography

1. Skinner, B. F. (2002). *Walden Two* (1. Aufl. ed.). München: FiFa-Verl

2. Our mission. Retrieved from https://www.health-right360.org/our-mission

3. African proverbs. Retrieved from http://www.myafricanow.com/best-african-proverbs/

4. African proverbs. Retrieved from https://themindsjournal.com/african-proverbs/

5. Africanproverbs.Retrievedfrom https://www.thoughtco.com/african-proverbs-and-quotes-2833008

6. Proverbs from Eritrea. Retrieved from http://www.madote.com/2011/07/top-10-greatest-eritrean-sayings.html

7. Proverbs from Eritrea. Retrieved from https://proverbsafricanliterature.wordpress.com/country-profile/east-africa/eritrea/

8. Class categories. Retrieved from http://udel.edu/~cmarks/What%20is%20social%20class.htm

9. Poverty. Retrieved from http://www.unesco.org/new/en/social-and-human-sciences/themes/international-migration/glossary/poverty/

10. Citizens united. Retrieved from https://www.history.com/news/14th-amendment-corporate-personhood-made-corporations-into-people

11. The NRA. Retrieved from https://home.nra.org/about-the-nra/

12. MIC. Retrieved from https://www.history.com/this-day-in-history/eisenhower-warns-of-the-military-industrial-complex

About the Author

 Bereket Abraha Negassi was born in Ethiopa in the mid 70's. When his beloved country achieved her independence after a thirty-year struggle that led to the recognition of Eritrea as a country, he officially became an Eritrean. Later, he and his wife moved to the United States and became citizens. They are raising three beautiful children here and feel blessed with everything they have achieved.

Bereket's formal education includes degrees in Human Resource Management, Natural Science, and Nursing. His informal education has been earned from talking to elders, reading books, and life experiences in Ethiopa, Eritrea, Kenya, Sudan, Egypt, and the United States. He has a lot of stories to tell regarding both his physical and spiritual journeys.

This heart-centered author is very thankful to have fulfilled two of his dreams. One was to visit Egypt; the other was to write a good book. It took him over two years to research and write Rectitude. It was presented at the 9th Annual CARD (Creative Activity and Research Day) and earned him the 2019 Academic Leadership Award from Vizuri Kabisa, the University of San Francisco's African American Student Union.

In addition, he was awarded the 2019 Dean's Medal for Promoting Professionalism from the University of San Francisco School of Nursing and Health Professions.

The author is grateful to have met many wonderful people at the University of San Francisco and at Walden House, which you will learn about in Book 1. Because of his experiences at Walden House, Bereket is donating 10% of the sales of this book to them.

59985861R00113

Made in the USA
Columbia, SC
11 June 2019